Poetry

CW01401867

2006

An Anthology of Four Line Poems on the Theme of Love

Published in Great Britain in 2008 by Aspiring Writers.

A CIP catalogue record for this title
is available from the British Library.

ISBN: 978-0-9558180-1-1

Typeset by Aspiring Writers.
Printed in the United Kingdom by Biddles Ltd.

Foreword

This anthology of four line mini-poems on the theme of love contains all the entries that filled the pews of St. Eustachius Parish Church, Tavistock, Devon for two weeks in February 2008. We calculated that 688 would fill the 86 pews and invited the local community to share their thoughts on the meaning of love. The project was organised to coincide with St.Valentine's day. Poems poured in from the local community (with over 200 from local school children), but also from all over England (Bury in Lancashire were particularly productive), Algeria, Australia, Canada, India, Italy, Morocco, New Zealand, Tasmania, Lithuania, Ireland, Scotland, France, the USA and Moldova. The poems were all laminated and placed along the ledges of the pews, choir stalls and on the church pillars.

We also organised a competition for those who wished to take part. The winning poems were as follows: Adult Winners: First Prize: No: 289 Mrs Dorothy V.J. Pope, Second Prizes: No: 174 Frank Woodcock, No: 139 Mary Beddall, Runners up: No: 193 Lorraine Dawson, No: 274 Lesley Woodcock, No: 704 Mrs Patsy Robinson, No: 1004 Ian Jenkins. Children's Winners: No: 16 Jack Childs-Watson, No: 564 David Farmer, No: 947 Melanie Zelinda Brown, No: 808 Mariah Calvert, No: 587 Ella Waddington.

The final tally of poems is 1063 + (+ because you will find that some numbers have an 'A' and a 'B' and so it is more than 1063). We were so overwhelmed by the response that we originally made some errors, but have chosen to leave the numbering in this anthology exactly as it was at the launch event on the 13th of February. The poems in this anthology are therefore listed numerically as they were displayed in the pews and not alphabetically. It was also decided that we would type up the poems and names exactly as they had been sent in. We felt that we had no right to alter or judge anyone's creative contribution. These poems are heartfelt thoughts and therefore technical perfection was not required.

We hope that you the reader will enjoy this collection. Some of the poems are humorous, some emotionally moving and others spiritual. Our congratulations go out to all those who had the courage to write, and share their thoughts with others from our

own community and around the world. We discovered love in all its aspects through this project, and it is without a doubt considered by all ages as a treasure to celebrate in creative words.
No: 70 in the Pews
Wouldn't it be great to hug the world,
To hold every nation, creed and race in a big embrace,
To say out loud 'I love you',
Because we are all part of the human race.

With our love to those who read this anthology,
Vanni Cook on behalf of the Poetry in the Pews Team
Tavistock, June 2008

Preface

I don't know if it applies everywhere in Britain, but certainly here in Tavistock, the local community looks to the parish church for a number of different things and in a number of different ways. The relationship is two-way and the parish church for its part, has developed a sense of service to the local community. This relationship is helped by the fact that we have a large and beautiful church building in the absolute centre of the town, surrounded by a churchyard, cleared of gravestones.

The relationship between church and community, like all relationships, needs investment - the taking of fresh opportunities to connect 'God' and everyday life and culture. I was therefore delighted when a member of our church congregation, Vanni Cook, suggested 'Poetry in the Pews' as a church project aimed at releasing the literary creativity of local individuals on the implicitly religious theme of love.

We were surprised at how the idea captured the imagination not only of locals, but further afield, and was taken up by national as well as local press. The glory of the idea was that the poems were restricted in length, which put all the entries on an equal footing, and enabled even the most hesitant writer to have a go. The number of entries far exceeded our expectations, and the project was enthusiastically launched on Valentine's eve.

I am especially glad that these poems are now being published. It not only confirms the gifts of authors, both experienced and inexperienced, but it also stands as a record of how a local church can engage creatively with the community in which it is set. I am extremely grateful to Vanni Cook and the team for all the work that they have done both on the original project and on this volume. I hope that this record not only brings fulfillment to those who participated, but also stirs other communities and churches to engage creatively with each other.

Michael Brierley
Priest-in-Charge of Saint Eustachius Church, Tavistock
21 May 2008

Poetry in the Pews Acknowledgements

Firstly we would like to thank the poets of all ages who made the effort to contribute their poems to this project.

We are also grateful to Elizabeth Cole (for all the laminating), Ann Pulsford (for 'badgering' so many people to write verses who had never written anything before), Sue Newman of Veritasse (for promoting the project), The National Poetry Library, Tony Giddings and Hilary Johnson (for encouraging local schools to enter), Jackie Waddle (for technical advice on printing), and to the judges of the poetry competition – Felicity Barnaby, Elizabeth Maslen and Patricia Fawcett. Without Kate Clough's patience and assistance fielding queries and acting, as postmistress at the St. Eustachius Parish Office the project would not have been possible.

Last, but far from least thanks to the congregation of St. Eustachius Parish Church, the Priest-in-Charge – the Reverend Michael Brierley and to those who provided the entertainment at our launch (All the readers, Flute Cocktail, Vocal Harem, Rosemary Turner and accompanist Mary Mazur Park and Maurice Sellick the organist). Not forgetting Jenny Metcalf and her team from the Friends of St. Eustachius who provided everyone with refreshments. A final thank you to Devon County Council whose funding will enable us to provide local schools, libraries and other groups with a copy of this community anthology for everyone to share and delight in.

Vanni (Myfanwy) Cook and the Poetry in the Pews Team

Devon
County Council

Poetry in the Pews – LOG

In a word
there are three things that last for ever:
faith, hope and love;
but the greatest of them all is love.
Corinthians 1:13

Name and Number for Pews	Place/Country
1. Elizabeth Cole	Tavistock
2,3. PS Cottier (2 poems)	O'Connor, Australia
4. Polly O'Brien	Belfast
5,6. Liz Verlander (2 poems)	Welwyn Garden City
7. Mrs Eileen Hooper	Tavistock
8. Hilary Johnson	Tavistock
9. Amy (Child 8yrs)	Bristol
10. Amy's Mum	Bristol
11-14. Jaydee	Bury
15,16. Jack Childs-Watson (10)	East Haddon
17. Cheryl Campbell	Luton
18. Sharon L Forsdyke	Leigh on Sea
19-22. Wendy Uzzell	Noss Mayo
23. Mrs Janet Monks	Tavistock
24. Ron Frazier	Portland, USA
25,26. Helena Ancil	Tavistock
27,28. Cedonia Lander	Torquay
29,30. Anna West	Tavistock
31,32. Jackie Waddle	Tavistock
33. Anna	Tasmania
34. Anna	Tasmania
35. Vanni Cook	Tavistock
36. John	Tasmania
37. Daryl	Perth, Australia
38. Jo	Perth, Australia
39. Joan	Tavistock
40 Joan	Tavistock
41. John	Tasmania
42. Wendy	Perth, Australia

43. Wendy	Perth, Australia
44. Wendy	Perth, Australia
45. Di Wilkie	Salt Lake City, USA
46. Di Wilkie	Salt Lake City, USA
47. Di Wilkie	Salt Lake City, USA
48-51. Jane G.	Southampton
52. Indie (Aged 7)	Exeter
53. Kat (Aged 12)	Exeter
54,55. Christian (Aged 15)	Tavistock
56,57. George	Bath
58-60. Ivor	Newport, Wales
61. Joanna Bone	South Brent
62-64.Tony	Dawlish
65-67. Janet N.	Plympton
68-70 Rose	Modbury
71. Carole	Birmingham
72. Steve	Plymouth
73 Cathy Towers	British Columbia
74-76. Mike	Bovey Tracey
77,78. Garth H.	Swindon
79. Auntie Liz	Tavistock
80. Barry Merryweather	Tavistock
81. Anne Witheney	Tavistock
82. Beth Cole	Tavistock
83. Eliza Duzlots	Tavistock
84. C&K	Tavistock
85. Annabelle	Tavistock
86. E.C.	Tavistock
87. Anne	Yelverton, Tavistock
88. Gladys	Tavistock
89. B.L.C.	Tavistock
90. EAW	Tavistock
91,92. Elspeth	Tavistock
93. Neighbour	Tavistock
94. C&K	Tavistock
95. EAC	Tavistock
96. EC	Tavistock
97. Liza	Tavistock
98. B.L.C.	Tavistock

99. A.L.	Tavistock
100. Elizabeth Cole	Tavistock
101,102. EW	Tavistock
103,104. EC	Tavistock
105. Elizabeth Cole	Tavistock
106. Garth H.	Swindon
107. Kirsty Matheson	Edinburgh
108,109. Phyllis W.	Tavistock
110,111. Elizabeth Cole	Tavistock
112. Lesley Woodcock	Tavistock
113-120 Ruth Daviat	Beddington
121. Ian Walkington	Tavistock
122. Mr. G. Spicer	Tavistock
123. Robin Start	Edwinstowe, Notts
124. Ian Walkington	Tavistock
125. Elly Cummens	Eugene or, USA
126. Ian Walkington	Tavistock
127-134. Michael Mates	Chisinau, MOLDOVA
137-143. Mary Beddall	Tavistock
144-155. Mrs B. Prescott	Tavistock
156-158. Ian Jenkins	Tavistock
159-168. Jan Robinson	Tavistock
169,170. Bet Kendall	Tavistock
171-175. F. W.	Tavistock
176. Peggy Cerbe	Glen Forest, Australia
177-181. Anna West	Tavistock
182-184 Rose-Marie Bonnevier	Tavistock
185-188. Pat Heppel	Plymouth
189. Mathew Jaquiery	Tavistock
190. M.A. Furze	Tavistock
191. Jessica Boatright (Aged 19)	Plymouth
192. Giedre Malinauskaite (Aged 19)	LITHUANIA
193-198. Lorraine Dawson	Bury
199. L.W.	Tavistock
200-203. Patricia Helen Robins	Newton Abbott
204-207. John Elinger	Oxford
208-215. Diana Mudd	Tavistock
216-223. Edna Eglington	Exmouth
224-235. Hilary Marsh	Peter Tavy

236-247. CJP Lee	Hatfield
248. Lindsay Sinclair	Bristol
249-252. Derek Taylor	North Hykeham
253-256. Angela Croft	London
257. Wendy Yelland	(DIY Poets Tavistock)
258. Patricia Bellotti	Manchester
259. Gill O'Halloran	Kent
260. Sue Newman	'Veritasse', Oxon
261,262. Sue Rowe	Tavistock
263. Sue Hawthorn	Horndon
264. Enid Williams	Tavistock
265. J.J. (N. Jarrett)	Faversham, Kent
266. Poppy Mitchell (Aged 10)	
267,268. Mary Norman	Green Valley, ARIZONA
269. Diana Brace	Tavistock
270-272. Jack Walker	Tavistock
273. Josie Brixton	London
274. LW	Tavistock
275. Shelia Armstrong	Tavistock
276-279. Michael Latimer	Witney, Oxon
280. Josie	Brixton, London
281. Veronica Aston	Tavistock
282. Kate Naokes	Reading
283. Mark Leech	Oxford
284. Patricia Ellen Curtis	Tavistock
285-290. Dorothy Pope	Harrow on the Hill
291-293. Isobel Thrilling	Romford, Essex
294-296. S. Williams	Berwick on Tweed
297-298. Roselle Angwin	Bere Ferrers
299. Mrs L. Foster	Plymouth
300. Mrs Mary Vague	Truro
301-302. Pamela Trudie Hodge	Plymouth
303-306. Mrs June Drake	Plympton
307. Joan Symons	Grenofen
308. Heather Warren (Aged 14)	
309. Mrs L. Radcliffe	Stoke Climsland
310-314. Ann Pulsford	Tavistock
315-321. Beverley Beck	Tavistock
322. Arthur Thomas	London

323-331. Pat Wright	Mary Tavy
332. Jack Walker	Tavistock
333-334. Ian Silcox	Tavistock
335. Rachel Burch	Tavistock
336. Robin Staplefcrd	
337. Elizabeth Cole	Tavistock
338-340. E sie	Tavistock
341. KC	Tavistock
342. EC	Tavistock
343. EW	Tavistock
344. Anne Teelle	Tavistock
345. Anne W	Tavistock
346-353. K.V. Skene	Oxford
354-361. Jan Robinson	Tavistock
362-371. Mervyn Prosser	Tavistock
372. Revc David J. New	Worcester
373-378. Germaine Knight	Ringwood, Hampshire
379. Rachel Green	Derbyshire
380-381. Sue Groom	Whitstable, Kent
382,383. M.Malins	Gunnislake
384. Phil Dyson	Gunnislake
385,386. Cynthia Richards	Tavistock
387-392. Myfanwy Cook	Tavistock
393-395. Bill Clacham	Isle of Wight
396-404. Pat Evans	Exeter
405-409. Mike Sadler	Plymouth
410. James Brookes	West Sussex
411-413. MC Smallwood	Texarkana, AR, USA
414-419. Uma S Jaiswal	Hadapsar Pune, India
420-425. Ian Jerkins	Tavistock
426-428. Joan Torvell	Tavistock
429. Mardi May	Perth, Australia
430-432. Ann Pulsford	Tavistock
433. Abi Martin	
434. Brie Burns	AUSTRALIA
435,436. Mrs K.Scarlett (Aged 87)	Plymouth
437. Stephen Roberts	Glastonbury
438. B.L. Lloyd	Bury
439,440. David Williams	Tavistock

441,442. Mrs F.M.Tindall	(DIY Poets) Tavistock
443-446. Julia Curry	Walkhampton
447-450. Patricia Helen Robins	Newton Abbot
451-457. Gwyneth Rosser-James	Wales
458,459. JC	Tavistock
460-462. Felicity Barnaby	Tavistock
463. Alison Dodge	Tavistock
464. Simi Chopra	Wolverhampton
465-473. Clare McCotter	Kilrea, N. Ireland
474. Janet Coopey	Okehampton
475. T.C.W. Stray	Davenport, IA, USA
476. Marika Linder	Bath
477-480. Shay Meredith	London
481-483. Professor Marsha L.Dutton	Ohio University, USA
484. Fran McMurray	Tavistock
485-496. Jean Symons	Horrabridge
497. Janice Lyons	Plymouth
498-503. Mrs Heather Grange	Plymouth
504. Sarah Wright	Northumberland
505. B. Martin	Bere Alston
506. Anon	
507. Sally Gethin	London
508. Trish Asman	Plymouth
509-510. Mrs Heather Grange	Plymouth
511-512. John Rea	Tavistock
513-517. Jan Robinson	Tavistock
518. Caroline Keane	Tavistock
519-521. Beverley Beck	Tavistock
522. Elizabeth Cole	Tavistock
523. Anne Withenay	Tavistock
524-525. Mrs. Melinda Mott	Plymouth
526. Seamus Harrington	Coastal Town
527. B.C.	Tavistock
528. Susi	Glen Forest, Australia
529. Stargazer	Tavistock
530. Sweetie-pie	Tavistock
531. Opera Lover	Tavistock
532. Cruiser	Tavistock
533. Easy Rider	Tavistock

534. Tim Haitch	Tavistock
535-537. Caroline Keane	Tavistock
538. Patricia Helen Robins	Newton Abbot
539. Wendy Shilson	Tavistock
540-545. EW	Tavistock
546-549. Beverley Beck	Tavistock
550. Maggie Thomas	Plymouth
551. Elizabeth Watkins	Tavistock
552,553 Sue Pesterfield	Tavistock
554. Rosemary Rea	Tavistock
555. Maralynn Butterworth	Tavistock
556. Linda Medland	Tavistock
557-558. Pam Hunter	Tavistock
559-560. David R.S. Melrose	New Maldon

St. Andrew's (Church of England aided) Primary School
561. Emily Spry (Aged 10)
562. David Carver (Yr6)
563. William Hassall (Aged 10)
564. David Farmer (Aged 11)
565. Oliver Straughan (Aged 11)
566. Amber Hardy (Aged 10)
567. Josie Flanagan (Aged 11)
568. Oliver Straughan (Aged 11)
569. George Carter (Aged 11)
570. Bryony Pearce (Aged 10)
571. Rosie Lloyd (Aged 10)
572. Josie Flanagan (Aged 11)
573. Rachael Kurdziel (Aged 10)
574. Penny Northmore (Aged 11)
575. Thea O'Callaghan
576. Jonathan Cull (Aged Yr6)
577. Rosie Lloyd (Aged 10)
578. Emily Cooper (Aged 10)
579. Penny Northmore (Aged 11)

Tavistock College
580. Amy Slowman (Aged 12)
581. Sarah Hornby (Aged 13)

582. A Deaglan Flynn-Samuels (Aged 14)
582. B Deaglan Flynn-Samuels (Aged 14)
583. Dani Gatcum (Aged 12)
584. Naomi Tucker (Aged 13)
585. Beth Standing (Aged 13)
586. Beth Markwell (Aged 13)
587. Ella Waddington (Aged 13)
588. Robyn Pinchen (Class 8DA)
589. Alexandra Guy (Aged 12)
590. Patrick Powell (Aged 13)
591. William Gardner (Aged 13)
592. Lydia O'Callaghan (Aged 13)
593. Christina Rowlands (Aged 12)
594. Eliza Austin-Hall (Aged 13)
595. Robin Lewis (Aged 13)
596. Will Hine (Aged 13)
597. Tessa Young (Aged 12)
598. David Walker (Aged 12)
599. Natasha Whiddon (Aged 15)
600. June Baxter (Aged 12)
601. Lucy Palmer (Aged 12)
602. Ollie Baker (Aged 12)
603. Michael Fisher (Aged 13)
604. Will Hall (Aged 13)
605. Sally Allison (Aged 13)
606. Sam Cooper (Aged 12)
607. James Woods (Aged 13)
608. Mathew Davidson (Aged 12)
609. Natasha Barrett (Aged 13)
610. Emma Cole (Aged 12)
611. Stephanie Credicott (Aged 12)
612. Kayleigh Edwards
613. Amy Ruth Bayliss (Aged 12)
614. Abby Emberton (Aged 13)
615. Mathew Bragg
616. Faye Wakley (Aged 12)
617. A Elliot Blatchford (Age 12)
617. B Elliot Blatchford (Age 12)
618. Theo Evans

619. Laura Taverner (Aged 13)
620. Tom Stoneham (Aged 13)
621. Lauren Martin (Aged 13)
622. Lily Fitzsimmons (Aged 12)
623. Jocelyn Mennell (Aged 12)
624. Laura Westacott
625. Laura Westacott
626. Laura Westacott (Aged 12)
627. George Conybeare (Aged 12)
628. Tierney Dower (Aged 12)
629. George Conybeare (Aged 12)
630. George Conybeare (Aged 12)
631. Tierney Dower (Aged 12)
632. Tabitha Crabtree (Aged 15)
633. Rebecca Tunnicliffe (Aged 12)
634. Luke Bailey (Aged 13)
635. George Fitzsimons (Aged 12)

More Poems from Adults

636. Tony Dunk	Tavistock
637. Jean Tarry	Bury
638-640. Mr. Martin Ullathorne	Yelverton
641-648. Julie Mellor	Sheffield
645-648. Aidan Baker	Cambridge
649. Josie Turner	Hitchin
650-653. Mary Roberts	Tavistock
654-656. Mary Hawkins	Tavistock
658-659. G.M. Saunders	Brentor
659. Jane Neeman	(DIY Poets) Yelverton
660. Joan Stewart	Tavistock
66. Greta Thomas	Tavistock
662. Justin Machin	Preston
663-665. Mrs Paulette Pelosi	Swansea
666. Crispin Williams	St. Ives, Cornwall
667. James Leonard Williams	Casablanca, Morocco
668-670. Margaret Wilmot	East Sussex
671. A. Key	Tavistock
672. Margaret Wilmot	East Sussex
673. Solomon Odeleye	London

674-676. Mrs Aileen SB Lobban	Edinburgh
677. Re	Algeria
678-687. Jean Symons	Horrabridge
688,689. AC	Tavistock
690. Jean Symons	Horrabridge
691. AC	Tavistock
692. Jean Symons	Horrabridge
693. GC	Tavistock
694-697. Kirsty MacDonald	Tavistock
698-701. Amenhotep	Tavistock
702. Christina Bird	Tavistock
703. Jean Vousden	Tavistock
704. Mrs Patsy Robinson	Petersfield, Hants
705. Caitlin Robbins(Aged 13)	East Twickenham
706. Lily Walke (Aged 4)	Tavistock
707. Anon	Topsham
708. Jean Symons	Horrabridge
709. Sandra McQueen	Dundee
710. Tim Jones	Tavistock

St. Peter's School – Tavistock
711. Hannah Greep (Aged 11)
712. Amy Collacott (Aged 11)
713. Harry Nicholls (Aged 11)
714. Oliver
715. Harry Cole (Aged 7)
716. Emma Nichols (Aged 11)
717. Nathan Turnock (Aged 11)
718. Kris Chapman (Aged 11)
719. Holly Gibbs (Aged 11)
720. Hannah Cox (Aged 11)
721. Nicholas Piper (Aged 10)
722. Nathan (Aged 10)
723. Zara Bartlett (Aged 11)
724. Beryl (Aged 11)
725. Kerry Watkins
726. Ethan Turner (Aged 8)
727. Jack Mathews
728. Joanna Bulley (Aged 7)

729. Mark Lewis (Aged 7)
730. Aaron Fry (Aged 8)
731. Callum Rule (Aged 7)
732. Ashling Heneghan
733. Harry Herman
734. Holly Kellock (Aged 8)
735. Francesca Herdman (Aged 7)
736. Sam Roberts (Aged 8)
737. Hannah Davenport (Aged 7)
739. Livvy Carr (Aged 7)
740. Ben Evans (Aged 8)
741. Aimee Tolley (Aged 7)
742. Carl Ellicott (Aged 7)
743. Joe D (Aged 7)
744. Lewes Hames (Aged 7)
745. Jacob Hawe (Aged 10)
746. Jacob Rawlings (Aged 9)
747. Alex Francis (Aged 9)
748. Emma Greening (Aged 10)
749. Grainné Fitzgerald (Aged 9)
750. Alex Williams (Aged 10)
751. Bethany Alford (Aged 9)
752. Rory E (Aged 10)
753. Martha Walke (Aged 9)
754. Lucy Miller (Aged 9)
755. Jessica Lillicrap (Aged 9)
756. Rachel Hooper (Aged 10)
757. Beth O'Boyle (Aged 10)
758. Barney Tossell (Aged 9)
759. Nathan Dodd (Aged 10)
760. Joel Gilhespy (Aged 9)
761. Angus F (Aged 9)
762. Myles Pinkney (Aged 9)
763. Callum Sherrell (Aged 9)
764. Joseph (Aged 8)
765. Megan Stone (Aged 7)
766. Marnie Hoare (Aged 8)
767. Alice Egan (Aged 7)
768. Anon

769. Kurt Goman (Aged 8)
772. Oscar Agnew (Aged 8)
773. Phoebe Woodhouse (Aged 8)
774. Daniel Hay (Aged 10)
775. Rebekah Hainsworth (Aged 10)
776. Millie Hames (Aged 10)
777. Jacob Early (Aged 10)
778. Tom Calvert (Aged 10)
779. Lucy Higgs (Aged 10)
780. Katelyn Dawe (Aged 10)
781. Martin Montague (Aged 11)
782. Lewis Brereton (Aged 10)
783. James Bartlett (Aged 10)
784. Cassian Bennett (Aged 10)
785. Jasmine Bartlett (Aged 10)
786. Kimberly Upcott (Aged 10)
787. Ben Hosking (Aged 10)
788. Ben Steel (Aged 10)
789. Shanelle Bowyer (Aged 10)
790. James (Aged 10)
791. Joseph Wheeler (Aged 10)
792. Adam D
793. Anon
794. Anon
795. Amy Lynch
796. Anon
797. J.Tolley
798. Jamie Toms
799. Emily MC
800. Anon
801. Jason Holland
802. Laura J. Fluin
803. Anon
804. Anon
805. Susi Benny
806. Lucy
807. Anon
808. Mariah Calvert
809. Anon

810. Caleb Prouse
811. Jack Veevers
812. Phoebe Sanders
813. Selina
814. Hannah
815. Jonathan
816. Adam
817. Aidan Evans
818. Millie Cox
819. Ellen
820. A Tate Budge
820. B Millie Steel
821. Caly Glover
822. Emily Pritchard
823. Laurence Harrison
824. Imogen Hollets
825. Richard Montague
826. Catlin Chapman
827. Daniel Cribbs
828. Amy Collacott
829. Isabelle Hall

More Poems from Adults

830-833. Anon	Tavistock
834. G.James	Wales
835. Jim Clements-Loftus	Redhill, Surrey
836. Lawrence Upton	Sutton
837-840. Gabriel Griffin	Orta, Italy
841. Marigold Rumble	Shaftesbury
842. Bettina Jones	Bury
843. Margaret Godsland	Exeter
844. VJP	Tavistock
845. Catherine Appleshaw	Andover
846. Oyinda Fakeye	Stanmore
847. M.Malens	Gunnislake
848,849 Brian Hicks	Tavistock
850,851. Christine Breckell	Plymouth
852. Cynthia Carpenter	Plymouth
853. Alex Street	Plymouth/Sweden

854. Lorraine Olver	Plymouth
855-857. Anne Everest	Sidmouth
858-867. Jenny Martin	Tavistock
868. Nola Venton	Plymouth
869. Anon	Tavistock
870,871. Joan Cheikh	Tavistock
872-876. Jan Robinson	Tavistock
877. Re	Algeria
878,879. Brian Hicks	Tavistock
880-890. AP	Tavistock
891-894. Sarah Pendle	Tavistock
895-899. EW	Tavistock
900-903. Beverly Beck	Tavistock
903. Jan Wilson	Horndon
904. Andrew Forrester	Horndon
905. Richard W. Halperin	Paris, France
906. Angela Kuchenbeck	Tavistock
907-910. Mrs Ros Knight	Buckland M. School
911-913. Anon	Tavistock
914. Seamus Harrington	Coastal Town
915-918. GMJ	Tavistock
919. Elizabeth Bennet	Tavistock

Lady Modiford's Primary School - Walkhampton

920. Louis Kirkpatrick (Aged 10)
921. Hugo Challis (Aged 8)
922. Emily Tidy (Aged 10)
923. Richard Cann (Aged 9)
924. Jacob Kirkpatrick (Aged 9)
925. Tom Eggins (Aged 9)
926. Ryan Brown
927. Carrie-Ann McDermott
928. Lee Thyer (Aged 10)
929. Alice Kodritsch
930. A Sophie Smale (Aged 9)
930. B Rebecca Steuart (Aged 10)
931. Mathew Jury (Aged 10)
932. Elliot Lister (Aged 9)
933. Daqlin Smart (Aged 9)

934. Floyd Ogle (Aged 11)
935. Adam Piper (Aged 8)
936. Joe Dyer (Aged 11)
937. James Anderson (Aged 10)
938. Tanya Wylie (Aged 11)
939. India Galbraith (Aged 9)
940. Nina Ives
941. Thomas Shipp (Aged 9)
942. Lauren Emony (Aged 9)
943. Tess Ashen (Aged 11)
944. Amelia Burnard (Aged 10)
945. Megan Groom (Aged 10)
946. Jake Woodgate (Aged 10)
947. Melanie Zelinda Brown (Aged 10)
948. Lily Spry (Aged 10)
949. Richard Young
950. Tommy Kalnins
951. Alice Neal (Aged 9)
952. Jade McDermott (Aged 11)
953. Ryan Shirlow (Aged 9)
954. Tom Christopher Robert Cooper (Aged 7)
955. Hannah Gordon (Aged 11)
956. Callum Mankoo-Bowers (Aged 10)
957. Callum Cunningham (Aged 9)
958. William Kirkpatrick (Aged 9)
959. Adam Thyer (Aged 10)
960. Mikey Ives (Aged 11)
961. Thomas Smale (Aged 10)
962. A Lauren Jane Gregory
962. B Molly John (Aged 9)

More Poems from Children

963-965. Morgan Buckley (Aged 6)	St. Rumon's
966. Shanelle Bowyer (Aged 10)	St. Peter's
967. Bradley Bowyer (Aged 5)	St. Rumon's
968. Jennifer Adkins	St. Rumon's
969,970. Victoria Heelis	Tavistock College
971. Rebecca Eldridge (Aged 12)	Tavistock College
972. Nicola Henerson (Aged 14)	Moffat, Scotland

973. Martha Walke (Aged 9)   Tavistock
974. Shayahi Kaithirgamanathan (Aged 8) North Harrow
975. Georgina Lloyd Owen (Aged 9)   London
976. Sophie Wildman (Aged 14)   Plymouth
979-983. Helen Radcliffe (Aged 16)   Stoke Climsland

More Poems from Adults

984. Raymond RJ	London
985-987. Christina	London
988. Jean	Bath
898-990. Felicity	Taunton
991. Elizabeth	Tavistock
992. Barry	Tavistock
993. Pip	Tavistock
994. Lily	Salisbury
995. E.C.	Tavistock
996. Katherine	Tavistock
997. Elizabeth	Tavistock
998. Harry W	Tavistock
999. PW	Tavistock
1000. Anon	Tavistock
1001. Mum	Tavistock
1002. E.W.	Tavistock
1003. Elle C.	Tavistock
1004. FF	Tavistock

More Poems from Tavistock College

1005. Alex Meyer (Aged 14, 10B)
1006. Rose Packer (Aged 14, 10B)
1007. O. Walters Meyer (Year 9)
1008. Ben O'Neill (Year 10)
1009. Dave Richards (Year 10)
1010. Mark Henderson (Year 10D)
1011. John Harley (Year 10DA)
1012. Louis Wilson (Year 10G)
1013. Ryan Bragg (Year 9T)
1014. Callum Coley (Aged 14)
1015. Alex Lecerf (Aged 14)
1016. Poppy Clark and Richard Coker (Aged 14)

1017. Jess Batten (Aged 13)
1018. Stephen Price (Year 9)
1019. Jade Collins (Aged 13)
1020. Jessica Quinn (Aged 13)
1021. Katherine Melville (Aged 13)
1022. Sophie Trudgill (Aged 13)
1023. Claire Fraser (Aged 12)
1024. Beth Kingman (Aged 13)
1025. James Brean (Aged 12)
1026. Lauren Evans (Aged 12)
1027. J. Woodhouse (Aged 15)
1028. Rachael Williams (Aged 15)
1029. Kirsty Woodward (Aged 15)
1030. Clara Wood (Aged 14)
1031. Sam Sills (Aged 14)
1032. F. Edgley (Aged 15)
1033. Leah Roberts (Aged 15)
1034. Ryan Smith (Aged 14)
1035. Kerry Horwood (9FA)
1036. Jack Litherland (Aged 14)
1037. Ione Geargakis (Aged 14)
1038. Ione Geargakis (Aged 14)
1039. Lesi (Aged 13) and Bradley (Aged 14)
1040. Chloë Boka and Katy Bennett (Aged 13)
1041. Jasmine Warne (Aged 12)
1042. Lauren Pike (Aged 12)
1043. Conor Hall (Aged 13)
1044. Fiona McCall (Aged 12)
1045. Chris Wilkie (Aged 13)
1046. David Watkins (Aged 13)
1047. Hannah Cole (Aged 13)
1048. Bethany Jade Dower (Aged 13)
1049. Kelly Walker (Aged 12)
1050. Mark Harris (Aged 13)
1051. Daniella Thyer (Aged 13)

More Poems from Adults
1052,1053. John Tunnicliffe   Tavistock
1054. S.E.N.   Tavistock

1055,1056. S.Rogers   Tavistock
1057,1058,1059. Ellie Madden-Crooby, Bridport
1060,1061. Astrid Fisher   Plymouth
1062. MIF   Tavistock
1063. Ian Jenkins   Tavistock

Poetry in the Pews - 2008

Life, Laughter, Learning, Listening, Leisure, Liberating, Leveller, Luminous, Lasting,
Oneness, Original, Opportunity, Observant, Outlook, Outward, Onward, Optimism,
Verity, Variety, Venus, Vital, Vivid, Versatile, Valour, Value, Vision,
Everywhere, Emotion, Energy, Enchanting, Exaltion, Everlasting, Eternity…

No: 1   By: Elizabeth Cole   From: Tavistock

Animals are us, writ in fur or feather.
Simpler, perhaps. But watch that bird.
Looping through space, an airy prayer.
And my dog? Smelly, but always there.

No: 2   By: PS Cottier   From: O'Connor, ACT, Australia

As you sit, reading, I'm nine hours ahead.
Here, on the stretching side of the world
it's often tomorrow. Australia's out of bed
while England sleeps. It must be the sun.

No: 3   By: PS Cottier   From: O'Connor, ACT, Australia

Columba was no angel and named both wolf and dove
The dichotomy of every heart
First he battled then he repented
An example to us all

No: 4   By: Polly O'Brien   From: Belfast

You and I had been together 40 years.
Then one sharp pain and you were gone.
I didn't speak for days nor eat properly.
But there it was-you were away with the fairies.

No: 5   By: Liz Verlander   From: Welwyn Garden City

Roses, scorched by autumn's matches, expose the prickly truth.
He is gone.
She avoids the window not wishing to face
Light in retreat.
No: 6   By: Liz Verlander   From: Welwyn Garden City

Within our intricate bodies,
Is sown a seed of love,
With infinite care it is placed there,
By our Heavenly Father above.
No: 7   By: Mrs Eileen Hooper   From: Tavistock

I wish that my nose would turn
Emerald when I am in love,
Then I would know
That it was true.
No: 8   By: Hilary Johnson   From: Tavistock

My Gran is great,
She bakes brilliant cakes,
She's got the time listen and play cards with me,
I love her and she loves me.
No: 9   By: Amy (Aged 8)   From: Bristol

Love is odd,
Sometimes you care for everyone with affection,
And sometimes it just isn't there,
I couldn't be like God, loving everyone, all the time.
No: 10   By: Amy's Mum   From: Bristol

When I look into your eyes, what do I see?
A bright glow and I know it's shining for me.
Your kiss goodnight, tells me there is no other
Person in this world, can love me like my mother.
No: 11   By: Jaydee   From: Bury

Compare love with a fine wine, they will mature given time,
Compare love with fires glow giving warmth as they grow,
Compare love and sun rays bringing long and happy days,
One love beyond compare, it's God's love for all everywhere.
No: 12   By: Jaydee   From: Bury

A man has followed me, for ten minutes I'm sure
If he hurries, I hurry more; I got to our corner
Then I feared the worse; he put his hand on my arm
And said, 'Ey are love you dropped ya purse."
No: 13   By: Jaydee   From: Bury

Church is a wonderous place filled with charm, grace,
Come inside, have a look, marvel at the Holy Book,
Admission to the Church is free. A welcome awaits thee,
Don't dwell in hesitation, come and join the congregation.
No: 14   By: Jaydee   From: Bury

Great relationship and understanding
Real Care and allowance
All this for nothing but the occasional hug
My Grandma
**No: 15   By: Jack Childs-Watson (Aged 11)   From: East
Haddon**

Mum of many talents
Other Mums cannot compare
Things like hugs are simple gifts
Everything you do for me is simply the best
No: 16   By: Jack Childs-Watson (Aged 11)   From: East Haddon

(Angel) A last cuddle
Then you were gone
But, we'll meet again
It won't be too long
No: 17   By: Cheryl Campbell   From: Luton

Pure Elijah lifts beams, swells hearts of mouth and ear,
Each perfect cadence satisfies the heart, makes all things equal.
Triumph and woe wear the same coat bestowed on sacred stones,
Giving fuller sound to life, ripening every listener to maturity.
No: 18   By: Sharon L Forsdyke   From: Leigh on Sea

A dog that greets you and jumps up with glee
On your arrival home, at the sound of your key
A child's smile as they meet you at the gate
No word of complaint even though you are late
No: 19   By: Wendy Uzzell   From: Noss Mayo

A mother's smile as a child runs a race
First or last there's the same warm embrace
As a father gives the hand of his daughter, the bride
A look that is sheer love and not only pride
No: 20   By: Wendy Uzzell   From: Noss Mayo

Love is not easy, no matter how it seems
We all must work hard to make the most of our dreams,
Love is a feeling, which lies deep inside
And yet it is not something that is easy to hide
No: 21   By: Wendy Uzzell   From: Noss Mayo

But when things are not going well
It's the love given to you
By family and friends
That helps to pull you through
No: 22   By: Wendy Uzzell   From: Noss Mayo

Love is here. Love is there.
Around a corner, in a prayer.
Open your eyes; see God's love all around,
Feelings of happiness in you will abound.
No: 23   By: Janet Monks   From: Tavistock

Inner peace is the principal characteristic of happiness,
We lose all inner peace when we become angry, depressed,
We stop being compassionate, loving, generous and forgiving,
The practice of compassion and love is the only way to inner peace.
No: 24   By: Ron Frazier   From: Portland, USA

The hollow tones of water on a jetty, slapping gently
Before the breeze. The golden Birch leaves dazzling in low
Sunlight, September memories were these. A dragonfly's reflection here,
Woos me to return Oh! Land of lakes and trees.
No: 25   By: Helena Ancil   From: Tavistock

November mist swathes the orchard. Skeletal trees bear solitary rooks.
Without warning, light melts the drabness, illuminating mouldering silvered leaves
Exposing glistening treasures. Birds seeking earwigs ravage the apples
Sheltering in winter's early rime. Savagely devouring Nature's autumnal plenitude.
No: 26   By: Helena Ancil   From: Tavistock

Faith she will come to me
Hope that she will stay
Love to last forever
And a day
No: 27   By: Cedonia Lander   From: Torquay

The musician loves his song
The writer loves her words
Artists love their colours
Ornithologists love birds
No: 28   By: Cedonia Lander   From: Torquay

Keep your passionate kisses
Lust rampant and wild
For there's no love as great
As the love for a child
No: 29   By: Anna West   From: Tavistock

Rich melting, delicious and dark
Stirred into cakes and frothy hot cups
Chipped into cookies and lush Belgian bites
I love it, sweet chocolate, sheer delight
No: 30   By: Anna West   From: Tavistock

Believe in me
And my tiny wealth
For no love can start
Without love for myself
No: 31   By: Jackie Waddle   From: Tavistock

Sensitive feelings, fragile states
Affection so patient and caring
Nurture life's loves to keep them all strong
Chase jealousy and hate into hiding
No: 32   By: Jackie Waddle   From: Tavistock

Voices singing in harmony,
Vocalising words of joy to delight,
Creating magic, relaxing the listener,
Expressing love infinite.
No: 33   By: Anna   From: Tasmania

Born in a stable,
No love could be greater,
A gift for everyone,
Love without question.
No: 34   By: Anna   From: Tasmania

Unafraid that he would fail,
A voice in the wilderness of life,
Born to give without expectation of repayment,
Bringer of Love amidst fear.
No: 35   By: Vanni Cook   From: Tavistock

Running away from love – impossible,
It will always catch you unawares,
The sparkle in a friend's eyes,
A touch from stranger's hand.
No: 36   By: John   From: Tasmania

Choir singing,
Organ playing,
Thrilling sounds,
I'm in love with music so sublime.
No: 37   By: Daryl   From: Perth, Australia

Dancing in a ring,
Holding hands,
Swaying, moving in time,
To the timeless melody of Loves' music.
No: 38   By: Jo   From Perth, Australia

Creativity,
Celebration,
Creation,
Love in Action
No: 39   By: Joan   From: Tavistock

What is love?
A friendly smile?
A gentle hug?
A caring word?
No: 40   By: Joan   From: Tavistock

Love can be oppressive,
It can curtail,
But it can also make the frail blossom,
Give heart to the weak.
No: 41   By: John   From: Tasmania

Sweetness, kindness are all expressions of love,
So are sharing and caring,
Any gesture that warms the human heart,
The finest type of love for me.
No: 42   By: Wendy   From: Perth, Australia

Rock the baby,
Welcome guest,
A treasurer forever,
The pure love and joy of motherhood.
No: 43   By: Wendy   From: Perth, Australia

A caress,
A kiss,
A sweet remberance,
Times past to treasure.
No: 44   By: Wendy   From: Perth, Australia

Hot chocolate,
Whipped cream,
Tastebud sensations,
Love without question.
No: 45   By: Di Wilkie   From: Salt Lake City, USA

Rocks, mountains,
Salt lakes and priaries,
All part of my country,
A place to love and cherish despite its faults.
No: 46   By: Di Wilkie   From: Salt Lake City, USA

Some people call me mad,
Some people call me honey,
Some people call me Mom,
Whatever they call me I don't care, I love them all.
No: 47   By: Di Wilkie   From Salt Lake City, USA

My daughter isn't easy,
She's going through the teenage years,
But despite the swearing, banged doors and angry tears,
I will always love her as she is my little girl.
No: 48   By: Jane G.   From: Southampton

My son is backpacking around the world,
I fear for his safety,
It worries me that I won't be able to comfort him,
My love is also my pain.
No: 49   By: Jane G.   From: Southampton

My husband wasn't very nice,
He loved his job,
He loved money,
But he didn't love me.
No: 50   By: Jane G.   From: Southampton

When you look into a person's eyes for the first time,
What are you looking for?
Is it appreciation? Is it approval?
Or is it to catch a glimpse of love divine?
No: 51   By: Jane G.   From: Southampton

I love Sandy,
He is white and gold,
He's the best hamster in the WORLD,
And he loves me.
No: 52   By: Indie (Aged 7)   From: Exeter

Love comes in many shapes and forms,
But the one that I love best,
Is a big hug from my Mum,
When life makes me really sad.
No: 53   By: Kat (Aged 12)   From: Exeter

I love music,
The heavenly harmonies,
The sounds drifting upwards towards the sky,
The joy and happiness it brings.
No: 54   By: Christian (Aged 15)   From: Tavistock

I love beavers,
Their small, nipping teeth,
Their warm fur,
The dams they call home.
No: 55   By: Christian (Aged 15)   From: Tavistock

The news depresses me,
Floods, famine, the despair of millions,
But then a flicker of hope and love crosses my mind,
God's light illuminates the unseen nobility of humankind.
No: 56   By: George   From: Bath

When we try hard and fail,
Our lives seem a mess,
But God knows we do our best,
God loves us despite the chaos we generate.
No: 57   By: George   From: Bath

Jesus could be gentle,
But wasn't meek and mild,
Jesus loved us as a good friend should,
He told us when we were out of line.
No: 58   By: Ivor   From: Newport, Wales

God's Love isn't water from a tap,
That we can turn on and off at will,
It's gushing out all the time,
And comes to constantly refresh our weary souls.
No: 59   By: Ivor   From: Newport, Wales

Eternal Love,
Acceptance without question,
Casting light,
Showing us back to where we came from.
No: 60   By: Ivor   From: Newport, Wales

Too many sweets can make you sick,
So can the wrong kind of love,
Love that demands everything and gives nothing,
Much, much worse for you than eating a tin a Quality Street!
No: 61   By: Joanna Bone   From: South Brent

Walking on the beach with sand beneath your feet,
It makes you understand,
That there are so many simple pleasures to love,
And that they are life's real treasures.
No: 62   By: Tony   From: Dawlish

When the wind lashes the waves against the sea wall,
When the seagulls hide from the storm,
When the rain hurls itself against the window,
I know how lucky I am to have my love to keep me warm.
No: 63   By: Tony   From: Dawlish

Sometimes I feel like a lone sailor,
Cast adrift on life's stormy seas,
But then I remember,
All my friends and how much they really do love me.
No: 64   By: Tony   From: Dawlish

What would we be without God's love?
It is that love that makes us hold out in times of strife,
That comforts us through our darkest nights,
And stills our deepest fears.
No: 65   By: Janet   From: Plympton

The menu of love is à la Carte,
Romance, Friendship, Family,
It's our own selection,
I'd like to think that everyone could sample them all.
No: 66   By: Janet   From: Plympton

You were a beloved friend of my childhood,
You weren't afraid to eat worms for a dare,
You didn't mind that you found reading difficult,
You died with anticipation of what came next.
No: 67   By: Janet   From: Plympton

I remember your Grandad,
He could tell a joke,
Always smiling,
He really loved everyone- strange that!
No: 68   By: Rose   From: Modbury

Family history is weird,
You find out about all these people, long dead,
You've never seen their faces,
And yet your kinship makes you love them.
No: 69   By: Rose   From: Modbury

Wouldn't it be great to hug the world,
To hold every nation, creed and race in a big embrace,
To say out loud 'I love you',
Because we are all part of the human race.
No: 70   By: Rose   From: Modbury

I can't help it'
I love chocolate,
It sweetens my life,
And definitely makes me more loveable.
No: 71   By: Carole   From: Birmingham

The love of my life,
Is my dear wife,
She is the living proof for me,
That God does exist and is looking out for me.
No: 72   By: Steve   From: Plymouth

There is romance in the air in Tavistock,
Seems folks down there they laugh a lot,
My darling and I will sit in the pews,
And be quite amused when they read out my views in Tavistock.
No: 73   By: Cathy Towers   From: British Columbia

The pinnacle of man's ability to create,
Roaring, hissing, fires by coal,
Built with love and care,
A Steam locomotive is beyond compare.
No: 74   By: Mike   From: Bovey Tracey

Some men dream of fame,
Others of a Porsche or expensive wine,
A wife and family may be top of their hit list,
But the love of my life is The Sir Nigel Gresley!
No: 75   By: Mike   From: Bovey Tracey

Hissing along the track,
Steam up, whistle bowing,
The Flying Scotsman hurtles by,
A romantic site to my mind's eye.
No: 76   By: Mike   From: Bovey Tracey

Can any woman ever understand?
The passion felt by an ordinary man,
For anything with four wheels,
In preference to two high heels.
No: 77   By: Garth H.   From: Swindon

A garage or a shed,
Created by god as man's earthly paradise,
A place to tinker with his car,
Bliss divine.
No: 78   By: Garth H.   From: Swindon

My sweet Great-niece said, "I love you",
It means the whole world to me,
For I know that this is really true,
Because she is not yet three.
No: 79   By: Aunty Liz   From: Tavistock

I love it when the weather's rough,
'pingy', hard rain, hail stuff.
I love it when the sun breaks through,
Radiant rainbows, colours true.
No: 80   By: Barry Merryweather   From: Tavistock

Love is a small four-lettered word,
That can bring warmth to your heart,
Lifts your spirit, lets your soul sing
And it encompasses everything.
No: 81   By: Anne Witheney   From: Tavistock

Real love comes from deep within the heart,
It sets the spirit free.
To others I shall love impart,
But first, I must learn to love me.
No: 82   By: Beth Cole   From: Tavistock

Diamonds are forever,
They have many facets.
A gem, a jewel, a ring whatever,
Love has many assets.
No: 83   By: Eliza Duzlots   From: Tavistock

A ring, a circle, never ending,
Goes right round the wedding finger,
Vows for life of love eternal,
Love for each other to last and linger.
No: 84   By: C & K   From: Tavistock

Ding, Dong! Wedding Bells,
Ring out for you this day,
Sing, Song! Anthems sung,
Love each other forever and a day.
No: 85   By: Annabelle   From: Tavistock

Nigella, darling power, flower,
Love-in-a-mist,
I will love you clearly, dearly,
Love is in our midst.
No: 86   By: E.C.   From: Tavistock

If music be the food of love,
Then I'll eat some in a minute,
'cos there's a ringing in my ears,
that's just a din in it, innit?
No: 87   By: Anne Yelverton   From: Tavistock

When I'm sad, I love my Dad,
When I'm glum, I love my Mum,
When I'm bothered, I love my brothers,
When I'm happy, I'm just so glad.
No: 88   By: Gladys   From: Tavistock

Love is being naughty
With a twinkle in the eye,
Love should not be haughty,
And never 'pie-in-the-sky'.
No: 89   By: B.L.C.   From: Tavistock

Love is a nurturing of nature,
Appreciating each moonbeam, each sunburst,
Every raindrop, tree, flower and creature,
Learning wisdom and knowledge with great thirst.
No: 90   By: EAW   From: Tavistock

God is LOVE,
Love is all around,
Only Love is real,
This is what I've found.
No: 91   By: Elspeth   From: Tavistock

Eternal love, I wish for you both,
As you make your wedding vows today,
For your two hearts to beat as one,
God guide, guard and protect you all I pray.
No: 92   By: Elspeth   From: Tavistock

I love horses,
I'd love a pony,
Would need a cushion,
'cos bum's so bony!
No: 93   By: Neighbour   From: Tavistock

Love today, Love tomorrow,
Love in sickness and in sorrow,
Look for the good and you will find,
Love is true, honest and kind.
No: 94   By: C&K   From: Tavistock

To love, you have to be loved,
To be loved, you have to love yourself,
To love yourself, you need to know yourself,
To know yourself, you should see yourself – Look Within!
No: 95   By: EAC   From: Tavistock

Wedding vows are about love,
And love is all around,
God's love comes from up above,
Seek and it is found.
No: 96   By: EC   From: Tavistock

I love you so much it makes my heart ache,
I love you with all my heart, for pity's sake
Hear my prayer and love me too.
Love me tenderly, Love me true.
No: 97   By: Liza   From: Tavistock

This ring of love, I give to you,
For you, I'll lay down my life,
This ring of love I give to you,
If only you'll be my wife.
No: 98   By: B.L.C.   From: Tavistock

This poem for you two as a pair,
To show you how much I care,
Forever in my heart with love you'll stay,
For all tomorrows, not just for today.
No: 99   By: A.L.   From: Tavistock

A wedding ring, a wedding band,
On third finger, on left hand.
Round and round and round it goes,
Encircling all the love it shows.
No: 100   By: Elizabeth Cole   From: Tavistock

I love my books, and how he looks,
I love my sewing, now he's crowing,
I love my pet, (oh, and the vet!),
I love the seasons, don't need a reason.
No: 101   By: EW   From: Tavistock

God's love, a parent's love, love is all around.
Sibling love, a child's love, these can all be found.
A love of nature, a love of all mankind,
A pet's love – unconditional love, seek and ye shall find.
No: 102   By: EW   From: Tavistock

Love conquers all. It comes from within,
Yet it can be a topsy-turvy kind of thing.
Through rose-tinted glasses, it's said, 'love can be blind',
Love is truth, honour, unconditional. Love should be kind.
No: 103   By: EC   From: Tavistock

Will you be my Valentine?
Has been heard over many a year.
Will you be mine?
Will you love me? Or do I shed a tear?
No: 104   By: EC   From: Tavistock

You should be here, by our sides,
On this Blessed Wedding Day,
For love gone past with time and tides,
Thoughts of you are never far away.
No: 105   By: Elizabeth Cole   From: Tavistock

Engines, cars and greasy things,
Spare parts the love of my shallow heart,
Glue, adhesive, solder what a treat,
Muck, grime and mess make my life complete.
No: 106   By: Garth H.   From: Swindon

A swallow in autumn flies away,
Chasing its destiny, to lands unseen,
And my heart migrates with it,
In the hope of finding you my one true love.
No: 107   By: Kirsty Matheson   From: Edinburgh

Love is many splendoured,
Love is many things,
I'll fly with you my darling,
With the wind beneath my wings.
No: 108   By: Phyllis W.   From: Tavistock

Will you be my Valentine?
Will you please be mine?
With all my heart I love you?
I hope you'll say, "I do".
No: 109   By: Phyllis W.   From: Tavistock

I love the trees in winter,
The soft sun shinning through,
Naked branches. Then
Hope leaves spring to life.
No: 110   By: Elizabeth Cole   From: Tavistock

I love to smell the damp earth after the rain,
See frogs and toads surface from hiding,
Watch raindrops gather into one down the windowpane,
The loving the sun that brings the majestic rainbow.
No: 111   By: Elizabeth Cole   From: Tavistock

(Rush Hour) On the crowded, silent tube
I smiled
Because I thought
Of you.
No: 112   By: L.W.   From: Tavistock

Affection resembles embroidery thread,
Enriching souls, silky svelte
and no less effective when no words are said,
with merely God's influence felt.
No: 113   By: Ruth Daviat   From: Beddington

She dallied distraught by the hospital bed,
Conscious of previous pain,
she'd caused with venom through bitter words said,
Loving too deep to explain.
No: 114   By: Ruth Daviat   From: Beddington

Shall I envisage whilst I still breathe
that friend with whom laughter is shared?
Will God permit that smiles once more wreathe
Our faces when love is declared?
No: 115   By: Ruth Daviat   From: Beddington

All I adore, my heaven on earth,
the blending by strings on the bow,
consummate chords a lifetime are worth,
fulfillment of all that I know.
No: 116   By: Ruth Daviat   From: Beddington

Tangible telephone, popular toy,
I put into use on a whim,
my heart somersaults for now I enjoy,
the sweetness, the ardour of him.
No: 117   By: Ruth Daviat   From: Beddington

We meet at seaside rendezvous,
exchanging views and warm embraces.
What equals such fine things to do,
with radiance of love on faces?
No: 118   By: Ruth Daviat   From: Beddington

As time advances, claims my vigour,
you, my daughter and your songs
enchant, my love grows bigger
and my heart with you belongs.
No: 119   By: Ruth Daviat   From: Beddington

Whilst music traps all waking thought,
annuals predominance of fear
once felt, entire my life is caught
and held, prevailing love draws near.
No: 120   By: Ruth Daviat   From: Beddington

Love is gentle, kind, forbearing,
Love is for our neighbours, caring'
Love is Jesus' gift for sharing:
Therefore, Join in Love.
No: 121   By: Ian Walkington   From: Tavistock

(KIS-MET) TWO PEOPLE, TWO LIVES, TWO HISTORIES,
ONE MISS-TURN, ONE FATE, ONE DESTINY,
TWO SOULS, ONE MEETING, ONE LIFE,
TWO HEARTS, BECOME ONE, MY LIFE
No: 122   By: Mr. G. Spicer   From: Tavistock

Love to love and enjoy people's cheer
Love to sample fine wines and beer
Love to hold our babies so near
Love to know that God is here
No: 123   By: Robin Start   From: Edwinstowe, Notts.

Love inspired our Saint Eustachius,
Faith confirmed his heart audacious,
Hope ensured his future gracious,
Steadfast for his Lord.
No: 124   By: Ian Walkington   From: Tavistock

Little ones grow like tended flowers,
Offering sweetness for nurtured care,
Verses tell us how Jesus loves them,
Everyone needs that embrace of God.
No: 125   By: Elly Cummens From: Eugene, OR, USA

Love is free – it knows no cost:
Without love our lives are lost,
Holy Spirit, Pentecost,
Give us all Your Love!
No: 126   By: Ian Walkington   From: Tavistock

86 collected pews
Tap the church's versing muse.
Each some lines on love displays-
This is how we'll count the ways.
No: 127   By: Michael Mates   From: Chisinău, Moldova

Eustachius is hard to rhyme,
But loves this rhythm everytime,
Patron Saint of us, Madrid…
I mentioned love-line 2- I did.
No: 128   By: Michael Mates   From: Chisinău, Moldova

Fill every pew, four lines of verse,
Concerning love and rather terse.
Unlike love, which lasteth long,
Eleven lines per line is wrong.
No: 129   By: Michael Mates   From: Chisinău, Moldova

Love is gentle, love is kind –
Keep the positives in mind!
But lest your mind be over broad,
Remember we've a jealous God.
No: 130   By: Michael Mates   From: Chisinău, Moldova

This is what I think of love –
It should fit like a glove.
Tight but supple it should be;
Ne'er let its contents wriggle free.
No: 131   By: Michael Mates   From: Chisinău, Moldova

Love is God, but love's not God –
Musings that you may think odd.
But if love takes too large a rôle,
How can the King be merely prole?
No: 132   By: Michael Mates   From: Chisinău, Moldova

Pelagian God and nice-nice man,
Both make love that's rather bland.
God Redeemer, sinful man,
Make a love beyond the grand.
No: 133   By: Michael Mates   From: Chisinău, Moldova

You must love it that I'm done,
And with my verse I've had my full.
Stick it on a pew or ten,
And say to versifier, 'When'.
No: 134   By: Michael Mates   From: Chisinău, Moldova

Does Christmas mean love and joy
And stars in children's eyes
The sense of wonder born of love
In Bethlehem that night
No: 135   By: May Carter   From: Tavistock

It's good to drink spring water
And breathe God's pure air
To see a smiling face each day
And not to have a care
No: 136   By: May Carter   From: Tavistock

I love to see the moorland sheep,
The gentle ewe, the noble ram;
Witness the annual miracle
That is the joyful Springtime lamb.
No: 137   By: Mary Beddall   From: Tavistock

You have to love the place you live;
If not, then all is out of line.
A town should of its essence give.
I'm pleased that Tavistock is mine.
No: 138   By: Mary Beddall   From: Tavistock

Love waits in the strangest places,
In dusty shadows, around dark corners.
You walk that way, unthinking,
And suddenly, the world lights up.
No: 139   By: Mary Beddall   From: Tavistock

You were so beautiful, so sudden,
An unexpected, searing comet of love
That, incandescent, flashed across my skies,
And then was gone.
No: 140   By: Mary Beddall   From: Tavistock

Where there's life, there's hope, they say.
Although you're lost, and dark the way.
The dawn will show you, before long,
Love in a flower, a tree, a song.
No: 141   By: Mary Beddall   From: Tavistock

Winter is the bleakest time,
Skeletal trees wild-flayed by freezing blasts.
But owls still love the icy touch of night,
And know that Spring will come.
No: 142   By: Mary Beddall   From: Tavistock

The farmer moves his sheep along,
Slowly through the glistening, frozen landscape,
And never wonders: "Is this Love?"
But it is.
No: 143   By: Mary Beddall   From: Tavistock

(V1) A sky of blue, the golden sun,
The busy bumble bee.
Flowers of all colours are such fun.
These are the things I love to see.
No: 144   By: Betty Prescott   From: Tavistock

(V2) Listening to the trickle of the stream,
The song of the birds in the air,
In the moonlight – the Owl's scream,
These are the things I love to hear.
No: 145   By: Betty Prescott   From: Tavistock

(V3) The scent of hay in the evening,
The bluebells in the Dell,
Honeysuckle – sweet and lingering,
These are things I love to smell.
No: 146 By: Betty Prescott From: Tavistock

(V4) Blackberries and strawberries growing wild,
Windfalls lying to waste.
All these I gathered as a child,
These are the things I love to taste.
No: 147 By: Betty Prescott From: Tavistock

(V5) A walk along the country lanes,
Explore the cliff tops too,
And squelching through the gentle rain,
These are the things I love to do.
No: 148 By: Betty Prescott From: Tavistock

(V6) Soft petals of the roses,
Furry creatures and the such,
Babies little pink noses,
These are the things I love to touch.
No: 149 By: Betty Prescott From: Tavistock

(V7) I sit a while and contemplate-
And count my blessings too,
For all these things I dedicate,
And give my thanks to You
No: 150 By: Betty Prescott From: Tavistock

(V8) Every Creature great and small,
From the beast down to the bee,
From the flower up to the tree so tall,
Are nature's family.
No: 151   By: Betty Prescott   From: Tavistock

(V9) Go out into the country
Breathe refreshing air
There's wonderment in plenty
For all of us to share
No: 152   By: Betty Prescott   From: Tavistock

(V10) For every newborn animal
What joy it is to see
And wonder at the miracle
Little lamb –who made thee?
No: 153   By: Betty Prescott   From: Tavistock

(V11) The perfumes and the colours
No human hand can make
Or imitate the contours
But only try – and fake.
No: 154   By: Betty Prescott   From: Tavistock

(V12) And who are we to put to test
The wonders of the world
For mother nature's way is best
Her banners all unfurled.
No: 155   By: Betty Prescott   From: Tavistock

Autumn winds blow sand and sea spray savagely though hair
With snow, the hungry birdsong breaks through chill winter air
In spring, the babbling stream will carry apple blossom smells
And warm long days of summer echo lazy tolling bells.
**No: 156 (Amour des Quatre Saisons)   By: Ian Jenkins
From: Tavistock**

A fragrant whiff which, instantly, sends nose and brain astray,
One tempting tasting, silken smooth, on lips will fleeting lay
But desperation, yearning more, shall be my piteous fate
Casting everything aside, in search of lovely chocolate.
**No: 157 (Fateful Fantasy)   By: Ian Jenkins   From:
Tavistock**

A fleeting glance, a glancing touch, a touching cherished word
These things we oft remember when past voices rest unheard
A pensive smile, a moistened eye, a whispered secret told,
Such pleasant memories, kept at heart, are treasures to behold.
No: 158 (Memories)   By: Ian Jenkins   From: Tavistock

(REAFFIRMATION) Kneeling beside you in the pew
Do we need to make our vows anew?
For twenty years we've both been true
And you know I'll always love you.
No: 159   By: Jan Robinson   From: Tavistock

(MARRIED LOVE) Now you are old and grey, dear,
No longer my beautiful bride
I love you even more, dear
Faithful and true by my side.
No: 160   By: Jan Robinson   From: Tavistock

(ANGEL) After a wait of many years
An angel came to me
A darling little grandchild
To snuggle on my knee
No: 161   By: Jan Robinson   From: Tavistock

(LOST LOVE) You are gone, my love
But I will never forget
You were my all throughout your life
Your spirit is with me yet.
No: 162   By: Jan Robinson   From: Tavistock

(WIDOW) Please don't call me Miz
Don't deny the man I wed
The many happy years we shared
And our love, now that he's dead
No: 163   By: Jan Robinson   From: Tavistock

(LOVE THY NEIGHBOUR) Who's my neighbour? The man next-door
Good or bad, rich or poor?
Now the world is held in thrall
To love my neighbour I must love all.
No: 164   By: Jan Robinson   From: Tavistock

(MY GARDEN) I love it in the springtime
I love it in the fall
But when the garden's full of bloom
I love it best of all.
No: 165   By: Jan Robinson   From: Tavistock

(SPRINGTIME) Sun-kissed, the cold earth cracks
Snowdrops burgeon forth
Tossing their white skirts in joy
Awakening love in spring.
No: 166   By: Jan Robinson   From: Tavistock

(LOVE MY DOG) I know you love my dog
Walking in sun and rain and fog
Caring, watching him run free.
Love my dog. Can't you love me?
No: 167   By: Jan Robinson   From: Tavistock

(WORDS) Logomania – I love words
Acrostic or in rhyme
Heteronym or anagram
I do crosswords all the time.
No: 168   By: Jan Robinson   From: Tavistock

(LASSIE)You obey my commands, no one else's but mine
Your faithful protection of me seems your task
My return home is greeted with exuberant whines
What love, my pet, what more could I ask.
No: 169   By: Bet Kendall   From: Tavistock

(GOD'S WEALTH) To love is to care, to give and to share
All that one has, even oneself
Real love can't end whatever it bears
It is selfless, forgiving, God's wealth.
No: 170   By: Bet Kendall   From: Tavistock

As time moves on
A quiet joy is discovering a new author
A real passion is finding
That the library has another twelve of his books
No: 171   By: Frank Woodcock   From: Tavistock

Love is when Madonna
dials your number
by mistake
then stays to chat for a bit
No: 172   By: Frank Woodcock   From: Tavistock

Actors rehearsing their lines on their own
Create mere sounds and gestures
But when they do it with others
Something magical can happen
No: 173   By: Frank Woodcock   From: Tavistock

I love the thoughts that go between words
As in a poem
I love the silences between the words
When we are together
No: 174   By: Frank Woodcock   From: Tavistock

Love is when there are no sweets
Or toys
Or other treats
But your son still hugs you
No: 175   By: Frank Woodcock   From: Tavistock

Softly on the grass I tread,
Delft - blue skies above my head,
Heat around, gum leaves falling,
Australian bush, my heart is calling…
No: 176   By: Peggy Cerbe From: Glen Forrest, Australia

No other musician has left his mark
Like the glorious supreme, only Bach
Hallelujah reaches every part of me
And I love each and every BWV*
No: 177   By: Anna West   From: Tavistock
(*BWV is the method of cataloguing Bach's works –
stands for Bach-Werke-Verzeichnis - Bach Works
Catalogue.)

Trees uproot to follow his sweet sound
Love with a nymph Eurydice is bound
A bite from a snake and from life she is hurled
Cast in death to Hades and the Underworld
No: 178   By: Anna West   From: Tavistock

Orpheus with his musical charm
Persuaded the dark king to undo harm
To rescue the nymph where his love lies
Take his sweetheart home with a compromise
No: 179   By: Anna West   From: Tavistock

Don't look at her yet, 'til the journey is done
He hears her behind him, her life he has won
Oh rapturous birdsong as he plays on his lyre
Eurydice won't keep up the pace and she tires
No: 180   By: Anna West   From: Tavistock

Impatience grows deep and his eyes play their trick
He turns on his love in seconds so quick
His lingering look is all to his cost
Death takes Eurydice, forever lost
No: 181   By: Anna West   From: Tavistock

"What is love?"
I asked my Dad,
"A tickle round your heart",
was what he said.
No: 182   By: Rose-Marie Bonnevier   From: Tavistock

Though everything in this world doth forward move,
The one certainty for a happier world, is love,
So, stand still, for just one moment of time,
And realize, all together, that true love is divine.
No: 183   By: Rose-Marie Bonnevier From: Tavistock

To love and be loved, is the hope of all.
So give & receive a smile with loving word
Let us go forward, loving standing tall,
Love is something that needs to be seen and heard.
No: 184   By: Rose-Marie Bonnevier   From: Tavistock

Words, what would we do without them?
No books to read, no writing to do!
The ones I would miss most of all,
The three that say "I LOVE YOU!"
No: 185   By: Pat Heppel   From: Elburton, Plymouth

God's love is all around us
On blossom, tree and flower,
What more do we want of life
But His embracing power!
No: 186   By: Pat Heppel   From: Elburton, Plymouth

Love is a many splendoured thing,
Love for parents, a soulmate, friend,
Love for the Lord who gave us life,
Mine to my spastic child He sent.
No: 187   By: Pat Heppel   From: Elburton, Plymouth

(The Rainbow) Never again would floods devastate Earth,
This is the Lord God's message of the rainbow,
When I see His coloured arc flash above,
I am assured of his promise and true love!
No: 188   By: Pat Heppel   From: Elburton, Plymouth

I saw you through the eyes of love:
Gargantuan and kind,
Then I saw through the eyes of love
And realised love is blind.
No: 189   By: Mathew Jaquiery   From: Tavistock

Love's battered blanket, flawed but strong,
Has warmed me through so many years.
Outside lie need and fear and wrong;
I'll raid my store to stem their tears.
No: 190   By: M.A. Furze   From: Tavistock

You are my happiness personified.
As you skip, your hair flows like golden streamers
When you breathe, butterflies escape from your heart
You are pure sunshine.
No: 191 By: Jessica Boatright (Aged 19) From: Plymouth

(Missing Love) We shared it all. In pieces.
Until now I can't fix myself. Puzzle parts are missing
Sometimes in the evenings I'm happy without you
Other times of the day I want you back.
**No: 192   By: Giedre Malinauskaite (Aged 19)   From:
Kedainiai, Lithuania**

Love is … A pewter cat like the brooch she'd loved and lost,
sought long and found at last by him in Halifax;
…A simple line in answer to her hurried note,
which ended "Love, Lorraine". "Certainly do", he wrote.
No: 193   By: Lorraine Dowson   From: Bury

(Happy Heart) My love keeps the beat
in my heart and dances on
in time with my feet.
Syncopated rhythm.
No: 194   By: Lorraine Dowson   From: Bury

(In Love Still) So we have parted
In love still without the will
to let the past go
and move on together.
No: 195   By: Lorraine Dowson   From: Bury

(Love to Live) I love those blue sky, glad to be alive days;
those sun-high, clear-bright, have to go outside days;
when you can taste the air; see for endless miles,
and the green limestone hills go on forever.
No: 196   By: Lorraine Dowson   From: Bury

(Recovery) When you strum love songs
my heart sings, remembering
when you were lost;
your sad days of silence.
No: 197   By: Lorraine Dowson   From: Bury

(A View to Love) We scrambled, breathless, to the top of Yr Eifl.
Excited, we held the moment, inhaled the view;
A priceless jewel for our chest full of treasure,
To take out and cherish, and polish with love.
No: 198   By: Lorraine Dowson   From: Bury

I have prepared your room for you.
I have made a cake and your favourite meal.
The house is warm, waiting for you to come,
And Jack will run to meet you at the top gate.
No: 199   By: Lesley Woodcock   From: Tavistock

To fall in love is passing wonder
But to be in LOVE: in that Silent Spendour,
Is to dwell in the heart
Of total surrender.
No: 200 By: Patricia Helen Robins From: Newton Abbot

(I RESOLVE TO) Do one loving act a day
Use wisely every word I say
Bless the thoughts with which I pray
Forgive the many times I stray.
No: 201 By: Patricia Helen Robins From: Newton Abbot

I love to dance, to play, to sing,
I love the joy such pastimes bring,
But to heal a bird of a damaged wing
Is, of itself, a loving thing.
No: 202 By: Patricia Helen Robins From: Newton Abbot

I love the sky, the wind, the sea
I love bread and jam and cake for tea
I love to know that friendship's free
But the hardest thing of all to love, is ME!
No: 203 By: Patricia Helen Robins From: Newton Abbot

Children play games: we adults work. We're even serious
About our sports – and sex! My reasons why I run,
Your solemn talk about true lasting love, they weary us.
Life is a game, and meaningless. Do it for fun!
No: 204   By: John Elinger   From: Oxford

Belief is not the same as superstition,
Conviction, or opinion. Faith is just
Like hope and love: a human disposition –
Explaining what we say: 'In God we trust'.
No: 205   By: John Elinger   From: Oxford

My friend's cv, he says, requires revision:
Another book? A grandchild? A new wife?
I face a much more difficult decision –
The need in my case is a change in life.
No: 206   By: John Elinger   From: Oxford

I love great cities: Sydney or Sienna;
Hong Kong, New York, the grandeur that was Rome;
Venice- La Serenissima, Vienna;
But Oxford above all, because it's home.
No: 207   By: John Elinger   From: Oxford

(Brief Encounter) Two minutes? Five? Twenty perhaps!
swirling emotions, stunned of mind:
speechless, numb and jelly-like;
so much, too much, yet not enough on such a brief encounter.
No: 208   By: Diana Mudd   From: Tavistock

(Live and Love) Live, and in the fullness thereof
you will Love.
Love, and in the fullness thereof
You will Live.
No: 209   By: Diana Mudd   From: Tavistock

(My Rosary) On my rosary I counted thirty-six beads
and, whenever you're away,
I send, on every single bead,
My love to you each day.
No: 210   By: Diana Mudd   From: Tavistock

(Love) In love, I beheld an angels smiling face
that gave of its all to beauty: with
a smile that bore its dedicated chores with grace, labouring
with undying love, its toil to deeds of duty.
No: 211   By: Diana Mudd   From: Tavistock

Love weaves its heart in threads so fine, so fine that only love could know what
grace the infinite bestows upon all those whose heart doth show and care enough
to freely give in dedication unto need, and, in its giving does commit, without
thought to any prejudice or creed to serve, with willing heart, each loving deed.
No: 212   By: Diana Mudd   From: Tavistock

(Dance with Love)
All the stars in the sky will dance with you
and the moon will glow in its highest heaven
when you dance with the tune
of love in your heart.
No: 213   By: Diana Mudd   From: Tavistock

(Time) Oh, what is time?
I care not what
If love alone
prevailed.
No: 214   By: Diana Mudd   From: Tavistock

(Love Outshines) Of all the stars that lend their sequined glitterings
to the excellence of a sparkling sky;
I clearly understand the reason why, and, in every thought of you recall,
That you outshine them all, for your love outshines a universe.
No: 215   By: Diana Mudd   From: Tavistock

(Restless) Like a free electron slipping an unstable bond
loosely combining with a passing crowd,
causing a reaction here, a current there, I find
if no love holds me freedom is lonely.
No: 216 By: Edna Eglinton From: Exmouth

(Safety Net) Love leaches through from heaven to earth,
reflects from earth to heaven. The world puts up umbrellas,
closes shutters, hides from the flood. Yet Love still flows
an endless stream that brings healing to the broken soul.
No: 217 By: Edna Eglinton From: Exmouth

Shall we make love? No. Love is not made
But given. Give love and find love
Leaching back replenished, to fill and overflow
That space left by the giving.
No: 218 By: Edna Eglinton From: Exmouth

(Dilemma) She is offended if I do not eat the creamy
gateau lovingly prepared. "We musn't waste,
eat up!" she says. I feel its weight upon my hips
and note the headline: FAMINE SPREADS.
No: 219 By: Edna Eglinton From: Exmouth

(Only Human) We pray for rain – complain of flood;
Long for sun – blister and burn;
Hunger for love- afraid to share;
And boast of our – discontentment.
No: 220 By: Edna Eglinton From: Exmouth

Slime drips emerald jewels from terrace to terrace
A garland of pimpernel sprawls over bottle and brick
Inquisitive dandelions thrust through corrosion of pram wheels
Mosses flow gentle as friendship to cover the waste
No: 221   By: Edna Eglinton   From: Exmouth

Silent in an empty church my heart found echoes ringing
From prayers of millions like wingbeats filling the air,
With love, joy, heartache, with knowledge, longing and care.
I add my own thanksgiving for finding a haven there.
No: 222   By: Edna Eglinton   From: Exmouth

(Seeking love)
children prattle universal greetings
smiles of mothers breach the culture barrier
travellers search each face for recognition
tears need no formal introduction
No: 223   By: Edna Eglinton   From: Exmouth

What you bring to me
Is Love.
A mirror-image of myself
That I don't yet see.
No: 224   By: Mrs Hilary Marsh   From: Peter Tavy

There's a reason that every hear knows.
Like a leaf tossed in the wind that blows
It drifts and dances, then falls distilled
To rest on Earth as Love that is willed.
No: 225   By: Mrs Hilary Marsh   From: Peter Tavy

Is Love in the blackest black, the whitest white,
In red and yellow, green and blue?
Is Love like the rainbow, a multi-hued light
That crowns both me and you?
No: 226   By: Mrs Hilary Marsh   From: Peter Tavy

Love is like fate, an intentional grace
Full of desire and ever there.
A willing without which I cannot be.
A life force by which I shall always be.
No: 227   By: Mrs Hilary Marsh   From: Peter Tavy

Being wise is a hard thing to be
And Love is a hard thing to do.
Because I am learning. I listen hard
To the wise things that other people do.
No: 228   By: Mrs Hilary Marsh   From: Peter Tavy

Love comes down at Christmas
Easter, Summer, Autumn too.
It doesn't matter who you are.
Only what you do.
No: 229   By: Mrs Hilary Marsh   From: Peter Tavy

A church is laid out like a man
(Or a woman, praise be!)
Arms outstretched and a heart at its heart
Just like you and me.
No: 230   By: Mrs Hilary Marsh   From: Peter Tavy

If you knew for a fact
That Love is always there for you,
How differently would you go about
Each daily act?
No: 231   By: Mrs Hilary Marsh   From: Peter Tavy

If I gave you a spark of celestial light,
Or a cooing dove to rest beside your head,
Would you love too the simple things I bring,
The ordinariness of home, the smell of homebaked bread.
No: 232   By: Mrs Hilary Marsh   From: Peter Tavy

Let us together touch the still point where God is
With Love devotional.
Let us bring forth the Love that God is,
In Grace and Truth inspirational.
No: 233   By: Mrs Hilary Marsh   From: Peter Tavy

Who, from the beginning, made your true self in Love?
Was it God?
Who, till the end, lives your true self in Love?
Is it You?
No: 234   By: Mrs Hilary Marsh   From: Peter Tavy

Ecoute, Dieu parle dans le silence*,
Escuche, Dois habla en el silencio
Hoere, Gott spricht in der Stille
Listen, God speaks in the silence
**No: 235 By: First line *L'Abbaye de St Martin du
Canigou, France (Mrs. Marsh) Peter Tavy**

She thinks about me all day of course
Especially when she walks home from school fortune telling
Kicking and deciphering the birdlike ochre and amber leaves
Their lines identical to the traces on her palms
No: 236   By: CJP Lee   From: Hatfield, Herts

God put away his compass
His trousers had so many pockets
He often forgot where things were so he had
Drawn a line around the world called the horizon
No: 237   By: CJP Lee   From: Hatfield, Herts

Adam's birthday party so we went to see 2001 AD
At the head of the table his older brother we had never
Heard of croaking incoherently at the bone hurled
Into space and morphing into our silent future homes
No: 238   By: CJP Lee   From: Hatfield, Herts

How pleasant she appears dressed as a man
Covered in 1940s cloth a real dapper dandy
Thick green wool razor sharp cut all now handy
With the supine egg gently perched on the neck
No: 239   By: CJP Lee   From: Hatfield, Herts

Something beautiful about London
In all its ugliness dressed or undressed like you
A man clasps his discarded heart
The throws it in the Thames
No: 240   By: CJP Lee   From: Hatfield, Herts

Turkish music floats over Golden Horn's shore
Pavements of Istanbul smothered vermilion
Vision from an album cover known and unknown
Now this is a case of love at last sight
No: 241   By: CJP Lee   From: Hatfield, Herts

Feather smothered field on London's cusp,
Your naked suburban fox licks paws leaves den
Stares across origin within our garden's depth
While cubs curl in lover's open nest
No: 242   By: CJP Lee   From: Hatfield, Herts

Through the oubliette lay the man's first wife stuffed
Like a baited bear with two bulbous glass eyes:
'That's to remind you of love,' cackled the devil.
'Or of knowledge,' croaked the divine looking monkey.
No: 243   By: CJP Lee   From: Hatfield, Herts

She loved to put lines through students' essays,
Whole paragraphs events in her recent past.
Like a fiddler who fails to replace string after string
Until she fiddles on nothing except her imagination.
No: 244   By: CJP Lee   From: Hatfield, Herts

I ask whether I can take the photograph now
Head jutting out as a freshly peeled onion
But the midwives discourage it electrodes long gone
Peace sweeping through as love on a January day
No: 245   By: CJP Lee   From: Hatfield, Herts

Art male 42 not bad looking – kind to his dog
Seeks WLTM younger Guardian reading voluptuous beauty
For the discussion of the finer things
Must not like Harry Potter
No: 246   By: CJP Lee   From: Hatfield, Herts

raise high the roof beams
over a hundred years of solitude
without we are lost drama the path
in case memory fails in case love is a lie
No: 247   By: CJP Lee   From: Hatfield, Herts

Sun shinning through your windows, giving a rainbow to enjoy
Everyone is welcome here, young, old girl or boy
To calm our minds, give thanks and pray
A special place in my heart, where you'll always stay
**No: 248   By: Lindsey Sinclair (LOVE OF A BUILDING)
From: Bristol**

(Dunham Church) Long deserted, left abandoned,
Jungled by the spreading trees,
Stonework mossed, grey, crumbling away;
A landmark now that no one sees.
**No: 249   By: Derek Taylor   From: North Hykeham,
Lincoln**

(Chapel Lane) Did Wesley ever stand upon this spot?
Did his sermons ever echo down this lane?
And today – when we contemplate mankind –
Do we own his mission triumphant or in vain
No: 250 By: Derek Taylor From: North Hykeham, Lincoln

(The Chapel) Built in faith maintained with love
By a congregation
Through sadness, elation –
Watched over from above.
No: 251 By: Derek Taylor From: North Hykeham, Lincoln

(Lent Lunches) Sipping soup in the schoolroom
Discussing weather,
Planting, sowing, how friendship is growing
In the garden they call Churches altogether.
No: 252 By: Derek Taylor From: North Hykeham, Lincoln

(The Wood) sunbeams filter through the leaves
a mist of bluebells
drifting under ancient trees
lingers in loves shadow
No: 253   By: Angela Croft   From: London

In the early morning, daffodils set the world alight
Primroses strew the path with kisses
The birdbath beckons the song-thrush and the lark
Here hops a tiny wren. Quick before it's off again!
No: 254   By: Angela Croft (Cottage Garden)   From: London

(Sunbeam) Cast your sorrows onto the waves as sunlight
filters through the leaded pains where we pray
The murals are faded but, though sadly decayed,
I se the faint trace of an angel there.
No: 255   By: Angela Croft   From: London

(Tea-Time) Lord of the spoons that mix a roux
stir a sauce, taste a stew, all have their uses
believe you me, but the one I treasure winks
from the dresser when the Vicar calls to tea
No: 256   By: Angela Croft   From: London

Love
Overcomes
Virtually
Everything
No: 257 By: Wendy Yelland (DIY. Poets) From: Tavistock

(The Love Bus) He drives the love-bus (passed the test first time),
Hangs about for ditherers, keeps an open door;
You pay him with kindness, friendship and a smile.
Where to? Who cares? – and there's room for one more.
No: 258   By: Patricia Belloti   From: Manchester

(Teen Spirit) I love to watch you walking away my love
Watch your rapture as you unwrap this world
Tugging at my dull wisdom like a kite unfurled
When the wind sings to it from above
No: 259   By: Gill O'Halloran   From: London

Love cradles the tiny babe, nourishing and protecting,
Over a bruised knee, love drops kisses; hugs fears away,
Vigilant when friends are cruel, supportive when hearts are broken;
Eventually, enduring love shows its strength by letting go.
No: 260   By: Sue Newham (VERITASSE)   From: Witney

Ancient market town on the river Tavy 'neath granite moors
your square is unique in its history and beauty
handsome Town Hall and Parish Church with open doors
there is no place on earth I would rather be.
No: 261   By: Sue Rowe   From: Tavistock

My gorgeous ginger gentleman means the world to me
and when I come home he greets me like royalty
with bright green eyes, bushy tail and silky soft fur
he fills my life with joy every time he purrs.
No: 262   By: Sue Rowe   From: Tavistock

We walk, wind whistling through the telegraph wires.
Silvered puddles, iced, still transformed by a copper sunset.
Warm and bronzed the alchemist works his magic.
Time for home leaving leadened ponds.
No: 263   By: Sue Hawthorn   From: Horndon

Seated quietly in my pew week by week,
I am told it is a Love poem they seek,
No hope, no literary talent of which to speak,
So sit back, listen to poetic verses and be meek.
No: 264   By: Enid Williams   From: Tavistock

(Flesh of my Flesh) In my aloneness, I'm not lonely.
In my loneliness, you keep me company.
Flesh of my flesh;
Blood of my blood.
No: 265   By: J. J. (N. Jarrett)   From: Faversham, Kent

There is a massive miracle in this life,
She takes my love into her heart deep, deep down,
And I love her every bit she could ever know,
Who is this it's the loveliest sister I could ever have.
No: 266   By: Poppy Mitchell (Aged 10)   From: Reading

Love is forgiveness unstinting,
Letting the past fade away,
Looking with faith to the future,
Living life fully each day.
No: 267 By: Mary Norman From: Green Valley, Arizona

Love is seeking God in other people,
Looking past the way they look and talk,
Channeling the grace so freely given,
Striving in God's footsteps thus to walk.
No: 268 By: Mary Norman From: Green Valley, Arizona

Cradled in the arms of my mother, I feel love.
Dancing cheek to cheek with my boyfriend, I seek love.
Cocooned in the chrysalis of my family, I find love.
Resting calmly at the spiritual centre, I am love.
No: 269   By: Diana Brace   From: Tavistock

(Love One) Love is lost
O Count the cost
View the scene
End the pride
No: 270   By: Jack Walker   From: Tavistock

(Love Two)
Lost in love
On a rainbow
Vision of delight
Earth is bliss
No: 271   By: Jack Walker   From: Tavistock

(Love Three)
Lonely for only
One day
Visit from you
Ended it
No: 272   By: Jack Walker   From: Tavistock

Love is –
A pair of jeans that fit,
A cake that isn't fattening,
A hair dye that covers every grey hair.
No: 273   By: Josie   From: Brixton, London

I have waited for you since the spring
When the blackbird sang in the apple blossom
But now he pecks at the fallen apples
And hunts for insects in the dead leaves
No: 274   By: Lesley Woodcock   From: Tavistock

Listen; can you hear the church bells ringing?
Organ music fills the air,
Voices from the choir are singing,
Endless joy and love; everywhere.
No: 275   By: Shelia Armstrong   From: Tavistock

As I journey through today,
Lend me guidance from above.
All I think or do or say
Be driven by love.
No: 276   By: Michael Limmer   From: Witney, Oxon

I seek no other path,
For He alone can guide me.
I need no other Friend
Than He who walks beside me.
No: 277   By: Michael Limmer   From: Witney, Oxon

The clamour of the world
Can have no purpose here.
I seek the still, small voice:
Lord, speak that I may here.
No: 278   By: Michael Limmer   From: Witney, Oxon

Your touch upon the world:
That it might turn again
And every hurt and bitterness
Be tended, soothed and healed.
No: 279   By: Michael Limmer   From: Witney, Oxon

I watch the television,
And see people suffering,
The only comfort I can offer is my love,
From deep inside my being.
No: 280   By: Josie   From: Brixton, London

(Glorious Devon) nose to the window as the river glides by
Whistles from the engine, smoke plumes in the sky
Sit back, smile, and give a happy sigh
Seeing Devon from a steam train is an 'anytime high'!
No: 281   By: Veronica Aston   From: Tavistock

(In the Drug Store) a stranger with tears in his eyes
asks me to hold his hand,
tells me the size of it as a cantaloupe.
I hold tight 'til his number is a called.
No: 282   By: Kate Noakes   From: Reading

(Firecrest) Colour on a thorn, turn-eye fixed on mine
Certain, twig-rider tensed, each featherpulse
Of her untuned song leading winter on.
Gone: the slow branch writes my love on the air.
No: 283   By: Mark Leech   From: Oxford

(Visions) I read of Ezra's visions, it excites me to know,
That people had such visions, all that time ago.
And people to-day, still have visions just as clear.
What an honour to know our Lord Jesus so dear.
No: 284   By: Patricia Ellen Curtis   From: Tavistock

(Hospital) Here's snowdrops' translucent beauty
to gladden your sad heart,
their seeming fragility
belying unexpected strength
No: 285 By: Dorothy V.J. Pope From: Harrow on the Hill

(Not Yet) Daily, his copy of The Times arrives
and I can no more cancel it
than I can bear to part
with his good overcoat.
No: 286 By: Dorothy V.J. Pope From: Harrow on the Hill

(Teaching) It's the light in the eyes
as understanding dawns
and clears the mists of misery.
That's what it is about.
No: 287 By: Dorothy V.J. Pope From: Harrow on the Hill

(Naturalist) and when he died,
two gardens to his credit,
he left the seed of his philosophy
in those who followed on.
No: 288 By: Dorothy V.J. Pope From: Harrow on the Hill

I gaze at my new sapphire ring
And see the cornflowers
That you gave me
In the kissing fields of youth.
**No: 289 (Forty-fifth Wedding Anniversary) By: Dorothy
V.J. Pope From: Middx**

(April) Quintessential and afresh, the primrose peeps,
its orange eye a-sparkle with held raindrop,
nestled like a clutch of eggs
in quilted moist green leaves.
No: 290 By: Dorothy V.J. Pope From: Harrow on the Hill

(North) Bird-note that turns me to glass
with its touch lest I shift a cell,
disrupt the pure mathematics,
mar the sound of a snowflake.
No: 291   By: Isobel Thrilling   From: Romford, Essex

(Snowdrop) Stalk aslant
in the dark wood
snags the
precarious tilt of light.
No: 292   By: Isobel Thrilling   From: Romford, Essex

(Healing) Forgiving is organic:
Seeds in the will, must penetrate
Bone and cell, removing dis-ease.
The body itself needs to heal.
No: 293   By: Isobel Thrilling   From: Romford, Essex

(Love of Creation) Gleaming dawn star
Shadowing silver moon
Fire setting sun
Crisp crunching frost
No: 294   By: S. Williams   From: Berwick Upon Tweed

Love is a tiny hand held gently in mine,
A beaming smile after a long day,
A short glance without words,
Laughter in the heart, through the soul.
No: 295   By: S. Williams   From: Berwick Upon Tweed

(Where will I find love?) Tell me
Where will I find love, for I do not know?
For thousands of years I have been searching.
Maybe I should stop and look on the inside.
No: 296   By: S. Williams   From: Berwick Upon Tweed

(January) I love rain in leaves, and thin sun sprinkling
the wrinkled winter creek where wild geese fly. I love
being here sheltered in the lamp's glow and imagining
a moment that these faces have only ever known light.
No: 297   By: Roselle Angwin   From: Bere Ferrers

(Leaf vernacular) How many years did it take, how much rain
and bone and sun, how much loss composted
into black peat to make this leaf, just this one
new leaf flickering green in the January ditch?
No: 298   By: Roselle Angwin   From: Bere Ferrers

(Love's Memory) My heart soared like a dove in flight.
Like a whisper in the dead of night.
A ray of sunlight dancing on a golden pond.
A memory of love, which then was gone.
No: 299   By: Mrs L. Foster   From: Plymouth

Love for the baby, love for the child,
Love for the teenager, troubled and wild,
Love for your family, stranger or friend,
And love the Lord Jesus, right to the end.
No: 300   By: Mary Vague   From: Truro

Wild moor beneath a silken summer sky
Eases the sorrow burdening my soul.
Gold fire of gorse, the skylarks' cheerful cry
binds up my ragged edges, makes me whole.
**No: 301(I Will Lift Up Mine Eyes) By: Pamela Trudie
Hodge From: Plymouth**

(Remembering You) You walked the lonely path from which,
they say, no traveller returns
but memories of you shine bright,
bright as the sacred candle burns.
No: 302   By: Pamela Trudie Hodge   From: Plymouth

During the day I enjoy writing poetry
Yet it's in the night that the best lines come,
Verse after excellent verse –
In the morning they are gone, quite gone.
No: 303   By: Mrs June Drake   From: Plympton

Our Church is packed into a small cupboard
Trundled out on Sundays in the Community Centre hall.
The real Church, people who are its members,
Are unconfined – they spread and flow with love.
No: 304   By: Mrs June Drake   From: Plympton

Our weekly Luncheon Club for Senior Citizens
Offers more than a reasonable priced good meal:
it's a social gathering where new friends can be made
and old ones enjoyed. You ought to hear the noise!
No: 305   By: Mrs June Drake   From: Plympton

She is grey, warm and lumpy, with undefined contours,
Makes you feel warm and welcome, quick to offer comfort.
Usually she is sweet, sometimes a little salty
But reliable and liberal to all: my porridge grandma.
No: 306   By: Mrs June Drake   From: Plympton

Love gives meaning to my life and showers me with its blessings.
Overwhelming in its beauty and purity, it transforms me daily.
Vigorously, it grows within me until it eclipses my selfishness.
Enveloping me in warm light, I am compelled to share it.
No: 307 (Love) By: Joan Symons   From: Grenofen

Love is a gift that all man has within.
It's stronger than any other gift that became in the world.
And like a child receives gifts from their parents,
We receive this gift from God for we are God's children.
No: 308   By: Heather Warren (Aged 14)   From: South Harrow

L. Let
O. Our
V. Valentine
E. Embrace
No: 309 By: Mrs. L. Radcliffe   From: Stoke Climsland

In an estuary of love we are stranded
Like leaves on the ebbing tide
Entwined lives are double handed
But our thoughts we can easily hide
No: 310   By: Ann Pulsford   From: Tavistock

Love is a dance
A quadrille of affection
A partner of chance
Can change your direction
No: 311   By: Ann Pulsford   From: Tavistock

Love is a word unspoken
A tender and caring glance
Faith and confidence unbroken
Someone to take your stance
No: 312   By: Ann Pulsford   From: Tavistock

Some people have a hidden beauty
A charisma and incandescence
They look beyond the line of duty
Spirits of enthusiasm and effervescence
No: 313   By: Ann Pulsford   From: Tavistock

We hope that the future will be like this
A romantic voyage on a hopeful craft
Our aim is wedded love and bliss
A relationship that is meant to last
No: 314   By: Ann Pulsford   From: Tavistock

(Glowing Amber) Glowing amber warms the sky,
Then slowly disappears from view.
Not to die, to be reborn
A miracle of love.
No: 315   By: Beverley Beck   From: Tavistock

(Gentle Flower) Gentle flower joy displays
Petals, stems, dancing seas.
Gentle flower sends a message
Love proclaimed, book of leaves.
No: 316   By: Beverley Beck   From: Tavistock

(Spring thoughts) As the raindrops
Coat each petal
With their love
The daffodils dazzle.
No: 317   By: Beverley Beck   From: Tavistock

(Awakening) A song bird startled me at dawn
His song loud and clearly heard.
A song composed, delivered, proud
A song of love, its voice referred.
No: 318   By: Beverley Beck   From: Tavistock

(How do I love thee?) Like the rain caressing the sea.
As a leaf enhances the tree.
As the petals on a rose open
And grow, so do I love thee.
No: 319   By: Beverley Beck   From: Tavistock

Gossamer threads cradle the raindrops
Allowing light to bounce from there midst.
Each tiny pearl a reflection
Of nature's kiss.
No: 320   By: Beverley Beck   From: Tavistock

(Recipe for life) In the store cupboard of life
Keep plenty of humour
An abundance of sensitivity
And lavish amounts of love
No: 321   By: Beverley Beck   From: Tavistock

The Bedford Hotel,
I love its scent,
The perfume of happy days,
Etched into its walls
No: 322   By: J. Russell   From: Bath

(Love is-) Loyalty comes in a shaggy coat,
Patience comes with eyes that dote
On the being coming through the door,
A simple love that will endure.
No: 323   By: Pat Wright   From: Mary Tavy

Friendship sprouts from tiny seed,
A smile, a word, a help in need,
With kindness watered and trust to nourish,
The gentle plant will surely flourish.
No: 324   By: Pat Wright   From: Mary Tavy

I beat my heart into the eggs and cream,
Breathed my soul into the golden froth,
Imagined your smile as you savoured the sweet,
And tasted my unspoken love.
No: 325   By: Pat Wright   From: Mary Tavy

Nothing delights my eye
As blossomed boughs against the sky,
Their petals falling in the Spring,
Like feathers from an Angel's wing.
No: 326   By: Pat Wright   From: Mary Tavy

And so we sat, and watched flames flare
As the wood fire spat, smoke filled the air
With yearning dreams inside my head,
But the longed for words were left unsaid.
No: 327   By: Pat Wright   From: Mary Tavy

Love is like the morning mist,
It evades the grasping fist,
But whisper gentle words of calm
And it will settle in your palm.
No: 328   By: Pat Wright   From: Mary Tavy

I wonder as I chop the wood,
What tree it was and where it stood?
I wish its atoms could create
Scenes of that forest in my grate.
No: 329   By: Pat Wright   From: Mary Tavy

You waved farewell, and the hands fell
Off the clock, the calendar froze
To a glacier of days no hope of thaw
Before you return, only friendless Winter.
No: 330   By: Pat Wright   From: Mary Tavy

Kings and Queens have been trapped in its devious spell
It promised them Heaven but turned to Hell,
Sometimes they swirled in ethereal delight
Soon to be spun into soul searing night.
No: 331   By: Pat Wright   From: Mary Tavy

(Total Love) Love is societies' gel, but only total love will do,
For inclusion must not become exclusion.
To give to one may be to take from another,
To love some should be the love of all.
No: 332   By: Jack Walker   From: Tavistock

(A Rambler's Song) I love and trust my walking boots,
Over mere and tor, cleave and moor,
Through tussocky grass and purple heather
What adventures we have had together.
No: 333   By: Ian Silcox   From: Tavistock

(An Erin Maid) an Erin maid at a dance I did see
Nearly fifty years now have wed
O what happy memories for me
Of that wonderful summer eve
No: 334   By: Ian Silcox   From: Tavistock

Oh my love, Tears stain my cheeks,
Our dream waves engulf me;
I will float on our memories forever,
Sweet gentle soul of the sea…
No: 335   By: Rachel Burch   From: Tavistock

I don't know who I am
I don't know what love is
I don't know who you are
But one thing is certain, I love you
No: 336   By: Robin Stapleford

Love is a 'gift',
It can be given and received,
Not just in the past or future,
But in the here and now, the very 'present'.
No: 337   By: Elizabeth Cole   From: Tavistock

I love your black wavy hair and deep brown eyes,
Your crooked bottom teeth when you smile,
Your warmth, comfort and the unconditional love you show me,
With just the wag of your tail!
No: 338   By: Elsie   From: Tavistock

Green eyes, amber eyes, watching where I go,
Dear constant friend, unquestioning, unwavering,
This much I know, how I love you so,
And unconditionally loved by you, waiting, watching, purring.
No: 339   By: Elizabeth Cole   From: Tavistock

My family is my life, my love, my all.
My friends are my chosen family.
The love, warmth and glow I feel for you all
Is so intense, it makes my heart ache.
No: 340   By: Elsie   From: Tavistock

Everything I do for you, I do with love.
It is the simplest, purest kind of love,
You love back implicitly,
Loving is such simplicity.
No: 341   By: K.C.   From: Tavistock

I love it when the sun shines
And helps the flowers grow,
I love the warmth and feeling fine,
This globe of yellow glow.
No: 342   By: E.C.   From: Tavistock

Giving out love
Makes me feel good,
It's like nourishment
That feeds the soul.
No: 343   By: E.W.   From: Tavistock

You are such a loving, caring,
Kind and thoughtful, sharing
Girl. That loving you
Is the easiest thing to do.
No: 344   By: Ann Teelle   From: Tavistock

Love is not just an emotion, it is everything,
It is hearing, smelling, seeing,
It is feeling, sensing, just being,
And I especially love to sing.
No: 345   By: Anne W   From: Tavistock

Life
can be beautiful
if you don't insist happiness
has to be fun.
No: 346   By: K.V. Skene   From: Oxford

Love
is more than an accident
waiting to happen
No: 347   By: K.V. Skene   From: Oxford

This poem
should not be read
by anyone
under 16 years of age.
No: 348   By: K.V. Skene   From: Oxford

(Daisy) let your petals flutter down
just
like
this.
No: 349   By: K.V. Skene   From: Oxford

Tears
like rain in spring
before the riot of summer roses, before
leaves fall again.
No: 350   By: K.V. Skene   From: Oxford

A soft summer night –
sings the dark –
each note pearls
a velvet pod
No: 351   By: K.V. Skene   From: Oxford

Listen
as nightmusic falls
like rain upon a desert. Listen
as each raindrop flowers stone.
No: 352   By: K.V. Skene   From: Oxford

Goldfish hang motionless
in dark pond water
lilies fold themselves
into sleep.
No: 353   By: K.V. Skene   From: Oxford

(Flower song) Snowdrops herald love in spring
Red roses show you're true
Dahlias blooming in autumn
Prove your love the whole year through.
No: 354   By: Jan Robinson   From: Tavistock

(Love food) I will grow you broccoli
Carrots, onions, salsify
Courgettes, potatoes if you wish
Blended with love, a tasty dish.
No: 355   By: Jan Robinson   From: Tavistock

(Music) If music be the food of love
I'll feast until I'm sated.
Classics, film-tunes, pop or jazz
It can't be over-rated.
No: 356   By: Jan Robinson   From: Tavistock

(Weather) Dropping intermittent rain
Clouds go scudding by
In a sudden shaft of sunlight
A rainbow smiles across the sky.
No: 357   By: Jan Robinson   From: Tavistock

(Nature) The wind in my hair, rain on my face
This surely is Nature's grace
Telling me that since my birth
I've been part of this bounteous earth.
No: 358   By: Jan Robinson   From: Tavistock

(Dartmoor) There's a piece of heaven in Devon
With standing stones and granite tors,
Tumbling streams, bracken and gorse
Sheep-nibbled pasture. It's Dartmoor.
No: 359   By: Jan Robinson   From: Tavistock

(Carpenter) The scent of freshly planed pine,
Curling the shavings round my finger
Smoothing my hand along the grain.
How memories of my beloved linger.
No: 360   By: Jan Robinson   From: Tavistock

(Faith) The lord is my shepherd, my mentor and guide.
Whatever I do, He's here by my side
He tells me to love my foes and my friends
And if I should fail, I must make amends.
No: 361   By: Jan Robinson   From: Tavistock

My love is like the driven snow,
As pure and pristine white as rime,
But, my darling, you must know
My love will never thaw with time.
No: 362   By: Mervyn Prosser   From: Tavistock

Our love is like a mountain stream,
Innocent, pure and crystal clear
And when we get too old to dream
Our love will still flow on, my dear.
No: 363   By: Mervyn Prosser   From: Tavistock

Time we know can sever,
All things not from above;
Nothing is for ever
Save God's abiding love.
No: 364   By: Mervyn Prosser   From: Tavistock

And what is love? I hear you ask.
Love is a person's life-long task.
But what IS love? I hear you say.
True love is GIVING every day.
No: 365   By: Mervyn Prosser   From: Tavistock

Love is like a pot-pourri
Of petals that would scent a bower,
Violets, pansies, hyacinths and
Every other fragrant flower.
No: 366   By: Mervyn Prosser   From: Tavistock

Love is caring, love is sharing,
Every hour of everyday;
We'll ensure our love will endure
For ever, come what may.
No: 367   By: Mervyn Prosser   From: Tavistock

Our love's not some romantic passion
Like star-shells bursting in the night,
Our love is gentle, soft and lasting
Our love's more like a candle light.
No: 368   By: Mervyn Prosser   From: Tavistock

When I first fell in love with you
I wondered: Will it last?
Today our love is just as strong
Though fifty years have passed.
No: 369   By: Mervyn Prosser   From: Tavistock

Haiku:
Love is not a dream
But a stark necessity
In a war-torn world.
No: 370   By: Mervyn Prosser   From: Tavistock

When all your plans had gone west
And your life had lost its zest
Of the solutions you chose to ease your woes
The love of a friend was the best.
No: 371   By: Mervyn Prosser   From: Tavistock

(LoveLine) He would phone the order through.
She would type each word he spoke. Until, one day, he
came to fetch the goods.
"So, you're the voice?" "I will," she said.
No: 372   By: Revd David J.New   From: Worcester

(My Shortcut) I have reason to believe the slow, slack,
stop, look back, steady plodding track of
time speeds up when you're around.
I may have found a shortcut.
No: 373   By: Germaine Knight   From: Ringwood

Shoulder to shoulder, in silence the rocks guard the shore.
Like ever-wed couples, they rest into each other's
Grey-topped shapes to watch the ebb and flow and
Leap and slap that will make them tomorrow's sand.
No: 374   (Shore to Love) By: Germaine Knight   From: Ringwood

Deep blood vision of tightly gathered moments
My sickness is vase-water descending, sinking
And I am red dianthus deeply drinking your
Compassion in a budding gesture
No: 375(Red Carnations)   By: Germaine Knight From: Ringwood

(Timing) Courage of a snowdrop to face the frost
Patience of hazel-bud holding its peace
Softening soil cradling the shoot
Jubilant bloom
No: 376   By: Germaine Knight   From: Ringwood

(Divinity) Sshh! Stay still now. Cradle that feeling
Like a baby in a hammock, be still now.
Feel the joy of oneness. Let it be, now.
Let it be now. Let it be.
No: 377   By: Germaine Knight   From: Ringwood

(Motherlove) Shall I sing feathers to snuggle you down in?
Shall you spill love for me to soak up?
Shall we laugh fibres to weave a hammock?
Let us tickle each moment into new births of motherlove.
No: 378   By: Germaine Knight   From: Ringwood

Heaven remembers
The contentment that comes when
Enfolded in wings,
Angelic.
No: 379   By: Rachel Green   From: Chesterfield

Like splintered emeralds, grass glints in sunlight, spiky as
hair on earth's crusty scalp, keeping it warm, waiting
for Spring to fling up prisms of pansies,
palettes of crocuses, kaleidoscopic tulips, like a well-watered rainbow.
No: 380(KALEIDOSCOPE)   By: Sue Groom   From: Whitstable

The joys of each make special this quintessential England.
Like the seasons, we may be envoy,
each to compliment the other. Beware Springtime,
she of all deludes we are younger than we are.
No: 381(WISHFUL THINKING)   By: Sue Groom   From:
Whitstable

When the master asked what would you like,
What did you answer?
When he touched your cheek and your heart sang.
What, but love, could be the answer.
No: 382   By: M. Malins   From: Gunnislake

Love awakens true desire and shows are hearts are singing.
Love, undaunted, seeks a way, in any situation.
Unpossessing, Love wants nothing in return for loving.
Love, unbounded, finds it has no need of limitation.
No: 383   By: M. Malins   From: Gunnislake

Birds in love are drawn to the skies;
The moon is faithful to the earth;
Eyes are held by joy in eyes:
These reflect what love is worth
No: 384   By: Phil Dyson (DIY Poets) From: Gunnislake

Hear friends now sitting in the pews
I listened to the nightly news
Join me and pray to God above
'Your tortured world enfold in love.'
No: 385   By: Cynthia Richards   From: Tavistock

The rain comes down all black and white
The room is warm – the fire alight
Through windowpanes awash I look
I snuggle down and read my book
No: 386   By: Cynthia Richards   From: Tavistock

Arranged marriages used to be all the thing,
A contract to support and obey,
To share life's circuitous route,
With a codicil for friendship and love to have its way.
No: 387   By: Myfanwy Cook   From: Tavistock

Umbrellas are like cupid's bow
They are a useful way,
To bring the shy together,
And hide first kisses on a rainy day.
No: 389   By: Myfanwy Cook   From: Tavistock

It's pouring outside,
It's pouring in my heart,
An inundation of tears,
As another love disappears.
No: 390 A   By: Myfanwy Cook   From: Tavistock

Two sisters,
Grafted together by time,
Harvesting the crop of their endeavours of love,
Over a slice of carrot cake and cup of tea.
No: 390 B   By: Myfanwy Cook   From: Tavistock

Love is an aerial act,
A tight rope tour de force,
One slip,
And your relationship is dead.
No: 391   By: Myfanwy Cook   From: Tavistock

Rain doesn't matter,
When your heart goes pitter patter,
Love makes you impermeable,
To the weather.
No: 392   By: Myfanwy Cook   From: Tavistock

Show me how you love me,
I know I'm more than a stolen cuddle on a summer's day,
I'm your alpha and omega,
I will be beside you forever and a day.
No: 393   By: Bill Clapham   From: Isle of Wight

Let me tell you of the ways I love you,
You are the crackling on my Sunday roast,
The sherry on my trifle,
The first sip of my best malt.
No: 394   By: Bill Clapham   From: Isle of Wight

To market I went,
And I found me a wife,
She cost less than a pig,
And now she's the love of my life.
No: 395   By: Bill Clapham   From: Isle of Wight

(Love) Love of people, much fun, love of music, singing done,
Love of animals, lick and bite, love of fashion, what a sight!
Love of colour, different hues, love of nature, super views
Love of children, is their right, love of God, faith alright!
No: 396   By: Pat Evans   From: Exeter

(The Lord) The Lord loves us all, even those who sadly fall,
Do not hesitate or stall, He will help, just call.
His love is all around, look and see, plenty found.
Hold hands from any lands, share a prayer, God is there.
No: 397   By: Pat Evans   From: Exeter

(Prayer) God will light the way, have faith, and pray each day,
In our darkest our He will give you power
To overcome troubles, like bubbles, disappear
All will be clear, to overcome temptation and fear.
No: 398   By: Pat Evans   From: Exeter

(Smile) A little love goes far no matter where you are,
You will feel a glow, your happiness within will show.
Kind words and a smile makes life worthwhile,
God's good grace will light your face, mile after mile.
No: 399   By: Pat Evans   From: Exeter

Smooth brows, wipe tears, give sympathy, dispel their fears
Invite homeless through the door, help the sick and poor.
We spend time helping each other, all people are our brothers,
Compassion and love, taught to us from God, above.
No: 400 (Comfort)   By: Pat Evans   From: Exeter

(The Vicar) in church to hear the vicar who is new,
I sat through his sermon, on a very hard pew,
The church was full, usually attended by only a few,
Approved, all who want to shake his hand please queue.
No: 401   By: Pat Evans   From: Exeter

(Self Help) Full heart and empty handed, intentions are all good,
Much chatter, toolbag clatter, little done, which could.
Made effort by one's self, put up badly needed shelf.
Of self-reliance brag, never again to nag.
No: 402   By: Pat Evans   From: Exeter

(Faith) Find a faith, believe in your Good to receive
Peace and love forevermore, say your prayers to be sure.
Use faith to lead your life, lead others away from strife,
Help those who lost their way, God is near, everyday.
No: 403   By: Pat Evans   From: Exeter

(A Garden) A garden pretty in bloom, beauty to lift the gloom,
In the air sweet perfume, please God, summer come soon.
We thank you for flowers, all insects and bees,
Tensions cease. in gardens fit to please.
No: 404   By: Pat Evans   From: Exeter

Wild sunset fills the sky
With luscious glowing cartography
Give yourself up to its spell
A moment in the mind of God
No: 405   By: Mike Sadler   From: Plymouth

Summer love- I recall and I desire:
Cool water thrilling down parched throat;
Shoe-bound toes set free to wriggle in the sand;
Mamma-sun's caresses melting my sorrows away.
No: 406   By: Mike Sadler   From: Plymouth

Said God, 'let there be Love.
At times you'll have problems how this should be used
Its magic may leave you aggrieved or confused
But it's great – well, at least it will keep you amused.'
No: 407   By: Mike Sadler   From: Plymouth

Love is like rain: in spring –fine refreshing, enticing;
Summer thunderstorms light up the night- power, rapture, surrender;
After that it's mostly drizzle really
(plus if you're lucky, an occasional flurry of twinkling
snowflakes)
No: 408   By: Mike Sadler   From: Plymouth

Sighing for Paris – boulevard café
Dreams stirred together – 'you're heart, s'il vous plait'
Bewitched by Montmatre, Notre Dame blessed
Memory – yearning – fantasy – quest.
No: 409   By: Mike Sadler   From: Plymouth

(Rogationtide) Light rain in a fallow season
streaks faces, fields and window-lead.
Summer peals on; the thunderhead
Breaks over the hillside – is gone.
No: 410   By: James Brookes   From: Nr. Horsham

The gorgeous hummingbird,
Your body like,
Drifts o'er your soul's lily,
Still snow-pure white.
No: 411   By: M.C. Small Wood   From: Texarkana, AR, USA

I feel Love in my bones but not my heart
For there is where you give me radiance,
In you, that final good and perfect art,
Between all lesser gifts and God's ma'jeunce.
No: 412   By: M.C. Small Wood   From: Texarkana, AR, USA

The elf I knew is with me still, so feels
The heart e'en on the storm-vexed seas of life
She's stronger, wiser, kinder, prove real –
No youthful dream, but storm-strong, steady wife.
No: 413   By: M.C. Small Wood   From: Texarkana, AR, USA

(Guru's Teachings) Life is the final play in a theatre;
Act truly from the first instance.
It isn't a tutorial dress rehearsal;
You will not get another chance.
No: 414   By: Uma S Jaiswal   From: Pune, India

(If God Went on Strike!) God makes concerted efforts,
Our gladness He loves to see.
To ensure no one is deprived.
He doles out goodies for free.
No: 415   By: Uma S Jaiswal   From: Pune, India

(Perishable Life) You praise the Lord while you can;
Life is perishable, not much worth.
The day will arrive for you to leave,
With no more but a fistful of earth.
No: 416   By: Uma S Jaiswal   From: Pune, India

(The Epitaph) A man sleeps here past his exile,
To end his life in domicile land.
The only life he was bestowed,
He failed to hold on in his hand.
No: 417   By: Uma S Jaiswal   From: Pune, India

(Traits of a smile) Smiley face is reminiscent of deity;
People will give up their attitude.
It's an emblem of heavenly traits;
Even animals prove their gratitude.
No: 418   By: Uma S Jaiswal   From: Pune, India

(What's the Good of it?) When one is tottering under pain
With profound suffering to utter;
Instead of offering personal help,
We ask the Lord to get him better.
No: 419   By: Uma S Jaiswal   From: Pune, India

(Solace) As quietly I sit here, for all the world alone,
Without a special partner, I come here on my own
But still I count my blessings, grateful thanks to send
For, when turning around and smiling, I recognize my friend.
No: 420   By: Ian Jenkins   From: Tavistock

(Together) I hear the gentle laughter, of those wed years before,
Who gathered at the altar, then processed to the door
Their lives were full of promise, joyful hearts with pride,
But now they rest together, asleep in ground outside.
No: 421   By: Ian Jenkins   From: Tavistock

(A Moor) Walking slowly through the heather, the tors before us rise
While soft rain gently patters down from multi-coloured skies
On reaching vantage points, we see around us heaven lies
A glorious scenic wonder on which to gaze our eyes.
No: 422   By: Ian Jenkins   From: Tavistock

She sits alone, aloof, serene, with elegance and airs
And all who pass admire her with envious longing stares
Her very whim is satisfied by friends and suitors, still
She rules the hearts of everyone, this feline queen, at will.
**No: 423 Cat as Trophy (Catastrophe)   By: Ian Jenkins
From: Tavistock**

(Racquets)I look my partner in the eye, desperately wanting more
Tension building, nerves on edge, we settle now the score
Dressed in white, she stands serene, dainty as a dove
But once again, the tennis match is lost-to love.
No: 424   By: Ian Jenkins   From: Tavistock

The squally breeze bows unkempt hair about my saddened face
As stumbling 'cross the field, I reach our special place
Where once we heard and watched the dawn
Give promise, snatched by death, and I am left, forlorn.
No: 425 (Lost)   By: Ian Jenkins   From: Tavistock

Love is. You and me, friends and family,
Yesterday, today, tomorrow,
Good days, bad days, and in between,
Throughout, bliss, joy and sorrow.
No: 426   By: Joan Torvell   From: Tavistock

Gazing on a new born, sun shining on the sea
A scatter of raindrops on a spiders web
A warm handclasp when feeling down
Are all expressions of endless love.
No: 427   By: Joan Torvell   From: Tavistock

A symbol of love, a smile from a stranger,
A prayer for a friend; a moment of giving,
Receiving a kiss, part of God's bliss.
Makes all our life worth living.
No: 428   By: Joan Torvell   From: Tavistock

Love smoothes my frowns and wrinkles
Ignores the dimpled cellulite
Love smiles at me with even dentures
And love makes everything alright.
No: 429   By: Mardi May   From: Perth, W. Australia

There was a handsome young vicar of St Eustachius,
Whose sermons were new and audacious,
But to give him his due he has filled every pew,
With writers and poets loquacious.
No: 430   By: Ann Pulsford   From: Tavistock

Poetry in the Pews - 2008

In this lovely parish church of St Eustachius,
We are about to make some poets famous.
Their poems on love should please those above.
And their readings we hope will entertain us!
No: 431   By: Ann Pulsford   From: Tavistock

St Eustachius! St Eustachius! St Eustachius!
This parish should soon become famous,
The poems, which we view, should fill every pew,
Long may their sentiments continue to sustain us.
No: 432   By: Ann Pulsford   From: Tavistock

Roses are red
His blood was, too.
Spilt on that day
For me and you.
No: 433   By: Abi Martin   From: Rickmansworth

In my small life there is a great truth, you
will never be lost. Walking on earth, my arms full
of roses, aware that you are near. When sweet, clean,
air touches the earth, I know it is you.
No: 434   By: Brie Burns   From: Mahognay Creek, W. Australia

My love is like a daffodil
That only blooms in Spring,
This card has been re-cycled
So it didn't cost a thing.
No: 435 By: Kathleen Scarlett (Aged 87) From: Plymouth

(Last Filing) He's standing on the patio
Throwing a little stone,
It's the only way to make me hear
When my daughter's on the phone.
No: 436 (V1)   By: Kathleen Scarlett (Aged 87)   From:
Plymouth

I didn't hear the doorbell,
But, then, my hearing's rather dim,
And I forgot 'twas Friday,
So I wasn't expecting him.
No: 436 (V2)   By: Kathleen Scarlett (Aged 87)   From:
Plymouth

He's too old to be a Romeo,
And I'm no Juliet
And if I don't look in the mirror
Age is easy to forget.
No: 436 (V3)   By: Kathleen Scarlett (Aged 87)   From:
Plymouth

I'm glad I put my teeth in,
And left my glasses off,
I won't see all his wrinkles,
And I'll try hard not to cough!
No: 436 (V4)   By: Kathleen Scarlett (Aged 87)   From:
Plymouth

At eighty, one is grateful
To entertain a beau
But, oh, I wish I hadn't
Lost my "get up and go"
No: 436 (V5)   By: Kathleen Scarlett (Aged 87)   From:
Plymouth

But I'll wear a dab of perfume,
And my lilac negligee
And pretend I'm only seventeen,
And he, a bold twenty.
No: 436 (V6)   By: Kathleen Scarlett (Aged 87)   From: Plymouth

(One year later) I shall not cry, there is no need for tears,
Rather shall I rememeber, our friendship through the years,
To all the good things in this life, there has to be an end,
Our flag of friendship is furled now, farewell my Friday friend.
No: 436 (V7)   By: Kathleen Scarlett (Aged 87)   From: Plymouth

(L is for Love) You asked if I loved you, I answered "I do"
and were I to measure this love for you –
it is high as heaven and even more wide
than all the angels stood side by side
No: 437   By: Stephen Roberts   From: Glastonbury

I hear the Tibetan wind-charm sound of boat hillyards
I see Dinghies in sandy bays waiting for the tide
I remember loved ones lying snug near a front wall
I love wide open skies awakening new visions and ideas
No: 438 (A Favourite Place)   By: B L Lloyd   From: Bury, Lancs.

(Coming Home –1) Cwm soft and all asinging,
Birds, tumbling water, trees,
Earth compelling, and sheep and sheeps
and she.
No: 439   By: David Williams   From: Tavistock

(Coming Home – 2) Slow, slow, dragons whisper,
stay contemplate awhile
the shepherd calls the sheep that roam
back home.
No: 440   By: David Williams   From: Tavistock

When you accept unconditional love
Your spirit warns and grows,
And from this transformation you will find
A need to share; and seeds of love to sow.
No: 441   By: Mrs F.M.Tindall   From: Tavistock

When my cat needs comfort and warmth
And chooses to sit on my knee
I know it isn't love he feels
But it's love I feel, and that's OK by me.
No: 442   By: Mrs F.M. Tindall   From: Tavistock

I poured salt on those flat slugs
and heard their pitiful screams
until love came to my garden
In the shape of a toad.
No: 443   By: Julia Curry   From: Walkhampton

(Me) I want my feelings to get hurt.
The thing that keeps me human
Is my vulnerability. It has led me
By the hand to find out who I am.
No: 444   By: Julia Curry   From: Walkhampton

(Lost Love) Love came, but lust
swallowed it up like
a green chameleon
catching flies with its long sticky tongue.
No: 445   By: Julia Curry   From: Walkhampton

(Recovery) Tears don't live in that beating drum of fear.
Tears don't flow from the whistling, screeching in my ears.
Tears don't prick at the pain stabbing in my back. No,
It's only love that causes me to weep.
No: 446   By: Julia Curry   From: Walkhampton

LOVE is reaching out when someone needs you.
LOVE is turning out on a cold night when you don't want to
LOVE is persevering when things try you.
LOVE is letting go when it hurts you.
No: 447 By: Patricia Helen Robins From: Newton Abbott

I wish I were in love again
All dewy-eyed and hazy
But then again, to live alone
Is to ear the right to be downright lazy!
No: 448 By: Patricia Helen Robins From: Newton Abbott

I look out on my garden in winter
Trying to remember what I've planted there
And I love to think of the long, hot days
When it is hard to remember my garden bare.
No: 449 By: Patricia Helen Robins From: Newton Abbott

I once made a vow '…to have and to hold…'
But where is my Valentine, now that I'm old?
He's not by my side as he once used to be
But I've found someone else to love – yes, it's ME!
No: 450 By: Patricia Helen Robins From: Newton Abbott

Love lines
Span the longitude
And the latitude
Of our life stories.
No: 451   By: Gwyneth Rosser- James   From: Wales

My mother loved her grandmother's
red flannel petticoats, which showed just a little
as she sat before the fire sipping tea
and exchanging gossip and sympathy- the Welsh Way.
No: 452   By: Gwyneth Rosser- James   From: Wales

I never knew my older brother,
He died a short time after he was born,
But I know his love surrounds me,
Reaches out when coal black days of hardship come along.
No: 453   By: Gwyneth Rosser- James   From: Wales

A kiss,
Friendship,
Loyalty,
Love's seals of respect.
No: 454   By: Gwyneth Rosser- James   From: Wales

Nothing nicer than holding hands,
Log fire roaring,
The embers of love glowing,
Dreaming of wedded bliss.
No: 455   By: Gwyneth Rosser- James   From: Wales

Our love of the Queen and her children is rather regal,
It comes from admiration and devotion,
A longing for the glorious past,
And sense that they are somehow family.
No: 456   By: Gwyneth Rosser- James   From: Wales

My father had a smiley face,
My mother gentleness and inner grace,
And the legacy they left for me,
Was their love for all, but especially for me.
No: 457   By: Gwyneth Rosser- James   From: Wales

My mother's strawberry shortbread,
Made with love as a birthday treat,
The smell, the texture all engraved,
and sweetened by time memory book of childhood delights.
No: 458   By: JC   From: Tavistock

A walk in the gardens of Versailles,
Icy winds wrapping themselves,
Around the young couple,
Embracing them in a wintry kiss.
No: 459   By: JC   From: Tavistock

Cerise and orange;
Sunsets flames the western sky
Quite magnificent.
No: 460   By: Felicity Barnaby   From: Tavistock

These I have loved: the glorious church,
The chattering Tavy, bubbling through the Meadows,
The purple moor standing sentinel over the town;
Tavistock.
No: 461   By: Felicity Barnaby   From: Tavistock

He was not widely known
Our patron Saint Eustachius.
But when the seeds of faith were sown.
He was, and stayed audacious.
No: 462   By: Felicity Barnaby   From: Tavistock

Vocal Harem meets at seven,
It is the ladies idea of Heaven,
Singing a variety of songs,
Although Rosemary knows we sometimes go wrong!
No: 463   By: Alison Doidge   From: Tavistock

With every high there's a low,
With every yes there's a no,
Behind every happiness there's a fear,
Behind every smile there's a tear.
No: 464   By: Simi Chopra   From: Wolverhampton

Dark blue censer
sky's benediction
first snow
augur of forgiveness
No: 465   By: Clare McCotter   From: Kilrea, N. Ireland

Lustral gold
suspended grief
descending
first falling leaf
No: 466   By: Clare McCotter   From: Kilrea, N. Ireland

Gnarled magi adoring
silver monstrance
mercury moon
wind-wept thorns
No: 467   By: Clare McCotter   From: Kilrea, N. Ireland

Each stone an urn
the scarlet bone dust
of departures
emigrants' cairn
No: 468   By: Clare McCotter   From: Kilrea, N. Ireland

Limbs of wh te gold
burnt sienna sky
stripped Calvary
the lightning tree
No: 469   By: Clare McCotter   From: Kilrea, N. Ireland

Gold and almandine
oblation -
fallen leaves
reconciliation
No: 470   By: Clare McCotter   From: Kilrea, N. Ireland

Suede river rose
colour of hope -
climbing
blue heron
No: 471   By: Clare McCotter   From: Kilrea, N. Ireland

Warmth underneath
a bay mare's
black mane -
the scent of silence
No: 472   By: Clare McCotter   From: Kilrea, N. Ireland

(Thakera) It is the aqua heart of a Palestinian night.
dust smells quiver on the road to Qalqilya.
you do not speak; the white moon is a frozen island
where our footsteps leave no sound, and always, the orange trees.
No: 473   By: Clare McCotter   From: Kilrea, N. Ireland

Ana behibak; Ami tomay bhalo bashi; Obicham te.
Arabia; Bengal; Bulgaria: meet love anywhere.
Bon sro lanh oon; Ljubim te; Miluji te.
Cambodia; Croatia; Czech Republic: give love everywhere.
No: 474   By: Janet Coopey   From: Okehampton

(So Little) All I know of love is complicated,
the longing, the want-delicious torment.
And craving of this thing, acceptance:
The belief that someone sees me, truly.
No: 475   By: T.C.W. Stray   From: Davenport, USA

(Concert) Silence; no one moves, everyone's still in
anticipation,
one note moves lonely through the tout ambience,
more follow, weaving too a large piece of music,
imposing it pervades the scene, the last note disappears; silence
No: 476   By: Marika Lindner   From: Bath

A bunch of gerberas
Red pink and yellow
In the hands of one woman
She breathes sunlight on this drab day
No: 477   By: Shay Meredith   From: London

I walk along the shore
And pick up seashells
Each one a dream itself incaptured
Each grain of sand has its story
No: 478   By: Shay Meredith   From: London

(Love-On Golden Wings) Make it winged
Make it light
Make it gold
Make it yours
No: 479   By: Shay Meredith   From: London

(Gazing) And I feel a certain power
A caring gaze
I feel safe
I feel listened to
No: 480   By: Shay Meredith   From: London

Silent as
the light that shone over
Bethlehem saving us from
the grave
**No: 481   By: Prof. Marsha L.Dutton   From: Ohio
University, USA**

Two hummingbirds drink
Deeply, at rest in midflight
Emerald passion
**No: 482   By: Prof. Marsha L.Dutton   From: Ohio
University, USA**

Last night I watched snow fall
On village street and square
Still today even here
He sends us snow like wool
**No: 483   By: Prof. Marsha L.Dutton From: Ohio
University, USA**

(Emergence) Once more I come into your room, deep down,
A basement, there cocooned and rocked to sleep,
In silken strands of love; When I emerge,
My colours show the light, or broken, fragile wings?
No: 484   By: Fran McMurray   From: Tavistock

I feel lonely,
Tonight is a Valentine party,
And, as I dress I hope to feel less
lonely tonight. Not more lonely.
No: 485   By: Jean Symons   From: Horrabridge

a tree dangles yellow catkins
against a river-bank of snowdrops.
a tree blossoms soft white pussywillow
against snow on the moortops.
No: 486   By: Jean Symons   From: Horrabridge

The snowdrops' white white light
At dusk, blurs in the gloom.
The streams' noxious mists boil,
Their unclean time comes night and morning.
No: 487   By: Jean Symons   From: Horrabridge

Where are you going to?
Take me.
What a lot of puddles you have!
You are a GOOD PATH
No: 488   By: Jean Symons   From: Horrabridge

Sop O be mine, O be mine, O be mine
Cont O be mine, O be mine, O be mine
Ten   O be mine, O be mine, O be mine
Bass Val ....   en...   tine
No: 489   By: Jean Symons   From: Horrabridge

Walkhampton Kissing gate
Meavy Kissing gate
Garden House Kissing gate
Roborough Estate Kissing gate
No: 490   By: Jean Symons   From: Horrabridge

Bob and Roger, pudding and pie
Kissed the girls 'O my, O my
proper job and proper job'
said all the girls, and Roger, and Bob.
No: 491   By: Jean Symons   From: Horrabridge

St. Eustachius
said, 'Goodness gracious!
now it's POEMS they choose
to peruse in the pews.
No: 492   By: Jean Symons   From: Horrabridge

my garden with small pink flowers
requires you be still alive
in your flat, in the far square.
my garden requires you there
No: 493   By: Jean Symons   From: Horrabridge

A sudden change in
your handwriting,
wobble,
of my whole being.
No: 494   By: Jean Symons   From: Horrabridge

Brush brush brush
Brush brush brush
Brush the stairs
with a hard brush.
No: 495   By: Jean Symons   From: Horrabridge

'Everyone' can't write a poem,
there is an enormous poetry world
and you have to inhabit it
to write a poem.
No: 496   By: Jean Symons   From: Horrabridge

(Birthday Presents) For a special birthday I was sent, a
Brand-new book; and an interflora planter;
Lavender slippers; and a bagpipe chanter!
…And love in the messages – concealed in the banter.
No: 497   By: Janice Lyons   From: Devonport, Plymouth

Stage Manager's last calls, violins re-tune, gold cloaks
shimmer,
Soloists and principals pirouette, a dancer's strap breaks.
Dancers await their cue. In the dressing rooms empty
hangers swing, dressers repair tutus. Degas is missing from the wings.
No: 498   By: Heather Grange   From: Peverell, Plymouth

On a torn piece of paper your name, address, fingerprints
Conjure up the two of us on a sunny afternoon
Promising to keep in touch. For you it was about
English lessons. Now I look at your handwriting instead.
No: 499   By: Heather Grange   From: Peverell, Plymouth

It seems like only yesterday, meeting in the Champs Elysées,
drinking tea in the rue de Rivoli,
working in a soup kitchen. It seems like only yesterday
I heard of your maladie. The 1980's – our heyday.
No: 500 By: Heather Grange From: Peverell, Plymouth

Traditions set a thousand years ago, stones especially laid,
worn, half exposed, like teeth until a torrent loosens them,
changing shape with the years, Why set out, why cross:
fear of what's upstream, or left dreaming on the bank?
No: 501 By: Heather Grange From: Peverell, Plymouth

(The Ballet) You sat behind with family and friends. In the interval
you slowly climbed back up the stairs. Our eyes met,
yours willed mine to hold the gaze. I looked away, felt you
grip the back of my seat. Nothing's changed.
**No: 502 By: Heather Grange From: Peverell,
Plymouth**

(Thé dansant) His arm around his partner's waist, the music strikes up,
pivoting on heels, foxtrotting, complicated side steps,
elegant, sedate, my grandfather's centre stage, where he wants to be.
Victor Sylvester's after tea.
No: 503 By: Heather Grange From: Peverell, Plymouth

(Missing you) I miss you in the dawnings of my days,
abandoning your fervent clasp in dreams;
although you keep your grip upon my heart
I'm loosely stitched together at the seams.
No: 504 By: Sarah Wright From: Northumberland

The truest of the many forms of love is Charity,
Loving the loveless with no thought of gain,
Exercised, it brings us close to Christ,
Where love is wrought from sacrifice and pain.
No: 505   By: B. Martin   From: Yelverton

(After Robert Burns) My love is like a red cherry cake
That's newly baked today
And I would bake again (for you) my love,
Tho' twere ten thousand cakes
No: 506   By: Anon   From: Tavistock

Let the tendrils of your hair
Fall soft upon your face
Let the sunlight casts its prayer
Upon your inner grace
No: 507   By: Sally Gethin   From: London

FOOD IS MY LOVE, I LOVE TO EAT
WHEN I FEEL LOW, I HAVE A TREAT
ALTHOUGH IT PUTS INCHES ON MY SEAT!
THE LOVE OF MY FAMILY IT CAN'T BEAT.
No: 508   By: Trish Asman   From: Plympton

(The Suitcase) Young, he left to fight a War. In the West
he worked in hospital kitchens, married, had children, kept bees,
loved gardening. When he died, well-thumbed photos, envelopes
lovingly licked down, a rosary, old keys, were thrown away.
No: 509   By: Heather Grange   From: Peverell, Plymouth

As the British Ambassador lays a wreath and ex-soldier,
Tears on his cheek, a French Countess be-ribboned,
Congregation button-holed with poppies stand to celebrate freedom
And when being close to death was heightened living.
No: 510   By: Heather Grange   From: Peverell, Plymouth

(Love Blossoms) I seek Love,
In a mist; in idleness.
I find Love
Lies bleeding: for me, for all.
No: 511   By: John Rea   From: Tavistock

Love affairs, love sick, love bites;
Love is cruel, love is blind.
Love endures, redeems, unites;
Love is patient, love is kind.
No: 512   By: John Rea   From: Tavistock

(Words of Love) My love is hard to put in words
It's difficult to tell
What my feeling's really like
Although I know it well.
No: 513   By: Jan Robinson   From: Tavistock

My love is like a poem
No reason but with rhyme
A simple rich emotion
That will last through time.
No: 514   By: Jan Robinson   From: Tavistock

My love's not a short story
There's no twist at the end
My lover, partner, helpmate
You're also my best friend.
No: 515   By: Jan Robinson   From: Tavistock

My love is like a novel
Which slowly will unfold
Fulfilling both our lives
Lasting till we're old.
No: 516   By: Jan Robinson   From: Tavistock

My love is like a library
Not just a single book
It's deep and all-encompassing
You enslave me with a look.
No: 517   By: Jan Robinson   From: Tavistock

Dashing young vicar, what more can they ask?
The ladies of Tavistock Church, to surpass
The Methodists, Catholics, 7th Day Adventists, too
Our Vicar's more dishy, and he sings better than you!
No: 518   By: Caroline Keane   From: Tavistock

Love is holding hands across a room
Of people who are distanced by time
Voluntarily touching and
Energising their receptive fields
No: 519   By: Beverley Beck   From: Tavistock

Letters combined form words
Often telling a tale which is
Variably distinct with
Emotions contained, word refrained
No: 520   By: Beverley Beck   From: Tavistock

Like all words this
One also suffers abuse
Various interpretations and use
Emotive, powerful four letters infused
No: 521   By: Beverley Beck   From: Tavistock

The sunflower is full of love and hope,
Showing strength in its magnificent height.
Its nutritious centre surrounded by an aura of yellow petals,
Its bold golden glow giving off wisdom, healing and light.
No: 522   By: Elizabeth Cole   From: Tavistock

Love in the world would make such a difference.
It would cross all barriers, bringing with it,
Friendship, hope, healing and wisdom
And everlasting peace and light.
No: 523   By: Anne Witheney   From: Tavistock

Friendship and fellowship; a lifetime of laughter
white dress and promises; happy ever after.
In the face of adversity; standing shoulder to shoulder
overcoming the sceptics; growing older and older.
No: 524   By: Mrs Melinda Mott   From: Plymouth

Poetry in the Pews - 2008

When certainty deserts you, where can it be found?
In the faces of loved ones, the compassion of friends?
Do you look to the heavens and into yourself?
and yes, there is love, can you feel it surround?
No: 525   By: Mrs Melinda Mott   From: Plymouth

(Regatta) Help us Oh! Lord to go straight
to where we're not looking
Steer us not into temptation
of looking where we're rowing. Amen.
No: 526 By: Seamus Harrington From: A Coastal Town

I love the peace in silence,
The nothingness and quietude,
The meditative me,
Nothing bold and brash and rude.
No: 527   By: B.C. From: Tavistock

When our dreams get diverted,
May our hearts make us serene,
As we wait for the right time of night
To dream and rise again.
No: 528   By: Susi   From: Glen Forest, W.Australia

The sun, the moon, the stars above,
These are the things that I love.
Leo, the Lion, the hunter, Orion.
And how about Neptune and Poseidon?
No: 529   By: Stargazer   From: Tavistock

Skittles are a knockdown,
Also sweets to chew,
They look like jewels from a crown,
I love them all. Don't you?
No: 530   By: Sweetie-pie   From: Tavistock

Songs from La Bohemme,
Rhymes like La Poemme.
Words are like a loving gift,
It gives the mind a certain lift.
No: 531   By: Opera Lover   From: Tavistock

All aboard the 'Love train'
Romance is in the air
Or we could have a cruise ship courtship,
Oh, I just wish I had the fare!
No: 532   By: Cruiser   From: Tavistock

Now here's a little ditty,
I thought it should be witty.
But what makes love so funny?
Just watch those Bunnies, honey!
No: 533   By: Easy Rider   From: Tavistock

Tennis is al about 'love'.
Love all, then play begins.
Singles, doubles, then forty love,
What the deuce? I'm in a spin.
No: 534   By: Tim Haitch   From: Tavistock

My love was like a dark red rose
With thorns which pierced and bled
So much for hearts, all pink and soft
I'll make more friends instead!
No: 535   By: Caroline Keane   From: Tavistock

From Abbey with Monks to plain Church with Hymns,
The old granite Church to its river banks clings,
We love this old Church with its' choir and its pews
Its peaceful location in Tavistock's mews
No: 536   By: Caroline Keane   From: Tavistock

From Tavistock Church on the edge of the moor
Comes music with stories and dancing steps, soar
To praise all the beauty, around us abounds
The glad heart of tidings, the joy of all sounds.
No: 537   By: Caroline Keane   From: Tavistock

LOVE is laughing at his jokes when they're not funny.
LOVE is buying him a present when you haven't any money.
LOVE is nursing him through 'flu, eyes and nose all runny
While staving off your own with lemon and honey!
No: 538 By: Patricia Helen Robins From: Newton Abbot

We sat together on the settee, Harriet, Rabbit and me.
'Rabbit has a name' said she, then silently gazed at me.
Percy I suggested, and waited expectantly,
'No Grandma, his name is Bunny' she responded scornfully
No: 539   By: Wendy Shilson   From: Tavistock

Please don't give me chocolates,
Please don't give me smellies,
I love to sit and read a book
or go out in my wellies.
No: 540   By: EW   From: Tavistock

The theatre is my love,
Acting, playing, singing.
Am I now to be a 'lovey'
And call everyone 'my darling'?
No: 541   By: EW   From: Tavistock

Bells ring out so joyful,
Telling the world your news,
The message is 'Just Married,
each other is whom we choose'.
No: 542   By: EW   From: Tavistock

I've loved you since first I saw you,
I'll love you for all my tomorrows,
I know you'll be forever by my side
and help me through all my sorrows.
No: 543   By: EW   From: Tavistock

I love the hat it's simply stunning,
Two-toned blue with flowers a brimming,
I hope the weather isn't cunning
So that they cascade into swimming.
No: 544   By: EW   From: Tavistock

The weather observer watches the clouds,
All the different heights, shapes and sizes.
Majestic elephant and castles in the sky,
Harps and hearts – love is in the air.
No: 545   By: EW   From: Tavistock

My heart is yours
You know it is
Passions soars
Each time we kiss
No: 546   By: Beverley Beck   From: Tavistock

The flower tilts her head
And listens to the bee
The butterfly fits from leaf to tree
A shady nook for you and me
No: 547   By: Beverley Beck   From: Tavistock

Melodious blackbird I would miss you so much
If you did not return to bring your babies to my table
Your mate to my door, and you, with your heart
Filled with love and so much more.
No: 548   By: Beverley Beck   From: Tavistock

Love speaks volumes
When it is allowed to grow
And so develop into what is sown,
We shall reap the more we sow.
No: 549   By: Beverley Beck   From: Tavistock

Oh how I love you so shiny and round
My heart beats with longing my love knows no bounds
I know you are wicked and will do me no good
But can I eat five crème eggs? Oh yes I could!!
No: 550   By: Maggie Thomas   From: Plymouth

(Cupboard Love) The upright tail, the weaving gait,
The upstretched face, the roaring purr,
The prodding paw on nylon legs,
"I love you, love you, love - but feed me NOW!"
No: 551   By: Elizabeth Watkins   From: Tavistock

As you grow in the Father's likeness
More like Jesus every day
May the glory of His approval
Be yours this special day
No: 552   By: Sue Pesterfield   From: Tavistock

Father, we are but dust
But when the Son beams down His Love Light
We glisten
And move toward the Light
No: 553   By: Sue Pesterfield   From: Tavistock

(Love is…) A little act of kindness
A wink from smiling eyes
A word of cheer, a listening ear
That's love in simple guise
No: 554   By: Rosemary Rea   From: Tavistock

I love this precious earth, these skies, these lands,
There is no known other to compare.
But now she must rest in our wasteful hands,
Yearning for a change we must all share.
No: 555   By: Maralynn Butterworth   From: Tavistock

One love, one man, one cross, one death,
One life exchanged for mine,
One hope, one faith in God above,
One Jesus – Love divine.
No: 556   By: Linda Medland   From: Tavistock

Love so tender,
With one kiss
I surrender –
Absolute bliss!
No: 557   By: Pam Hunter   From: Tavistock

Now love is gone, promises broken,
Words said that would better be unspoken.
Once so beautiful and new, now empty and cold,
Memories tarnished, dreams never to unfold.
No: 558   By: Pam Hunter   From: Tavistock

I see you on the guard rail of your life
Between safety and the deep
God watch and keep you safe I pray,
Until the next time we all meet
No: 559   By: David R.S. Melrose   From: New Malden

She smiled when I left her
Tonight there are no stars in the skies
No reprise
No: 560   By: David R.S. Melrose   From: New Malden

**Poems from St. Andrew's (Church of England aided)
Primary School, Buckland Monachorum**

Love is mysterious,
Love is divine,
Love is precious,
On Valentine.
No: 561   By: Emily Spry   (Aged 10)

Love is amazing
always changing
love is a mystery
making the world turn round.
No: 562   By: David Carver   (Year 6)

Love is powerful,
Love is great,
come on everyone,
call it your mate.
No: 563   By: William Hassall   (Year 6)

Love is a volcano:
It erupts and spreads its power;
A red hot molten glow,
That melts your heart.
No: 564   By: David Farmer   (Aged 11)

Love is amazing,
And is blazing,
And in our lives,
It goes on and flies.
No: 565   By: Oliver Straughan   (Aged 11)

In flew a dove
Which filled the world with love
Filling the world with peace
Making it a happy place
No: 566   By: Amber Hardy   (Aged 10)

Love is always in the air
Falling over you
Like a gentle rain fall
Spreading goodness to you
No: 567   By: Josie Flanagan   (Aged 11)

Love is a Mystery,
How it makes you think,
Love is magnificent,
It makes you feel great.
No: 568   By: Oliver Straughan   (Aged 11)

There was a feeling called love,
That was signalled by the sign of a dove,
Love is so bright,
And it shines like a light.
No: 569   By: George Carter   (Aged 11)

The world is crying,
The world is dying,
So give it a hug,
And show some love!
No: 570   By: Bryony Pearce   (Aged 10)

Love is a precious gift,
How it will gently lift,
You up into the sky,
Where you feel you can fly.
No: 571   By: Rosie Lloyd   (Aged 10)

Everyone has love inside them
Everyone needs love for life,
It doesn't matter who you are
Love will never end.
No: 572   By: Josie Flanagan   (Aged 11)

Love makes the world go round,
Love is in everyone.
Love is in your heart,
Love makes the world go round.
No: 573   By: Rachael Kurdziel   (Aged 10)

Love is like a mountain
When you get there it's amazing
It lifts you up into the sky
But to get there-it's a challenge!
No: 574   By: Penny Northmore   (Aged 11)

Everyone Loves Somebody,
I Love, You Love, Everyone Loves,
Even if you don't think you Love,
Deep down your heart belongs to somebody!
No: 575   By: Thea O'Callaghan   (Year 6)

Love is mysterious,
Love is devious,
Love makes the world go round,
Right to the bottom of the ground.
No: 576   By: Jonathan Cull   (Year 6)

Love's what makes the world go round.
People jump at the sound,
Of a new friend to be made,
Love's not something to be paid.
No: 577   By: Rosie Ward   (Aged 10)

Love heals all the pain
That makes you happy again
Love is your best friend
Love never ends
No: 578   By: Emily Cooper   (Aged 10)

Up from above
Came a lovely dove
That brought peace on earth
and showed us what we're worth
No: 579   By: Penny Northmore   (Aged 11)

Poems from Tavistock College

Love is like Music,
you get caught in the beat,
you feel the rhythm,
in the sweet summer heat.
No: 580   By: Amy Slowman   (Aged 12)

Love is a net,
You get caught like a fish,
Struggling to meet the one that you wish,
Waiting for true love's first kiss.
No: 581   By: Sarah Hornby   (Aged 13)

My Bedroom
A Place of Safety
A Place to go in times of need
A Place where I can let go of everything
No: 582 A   By: Deaglan Flynn-Samuels   (Aged 14)

Winter (The crunch of snow beneath my feet
The frost glistening on the trees
Blankets of pure white wherever I look
Children playing in the streets
No: 582 B   By: Deaglan Flynn-Samuels   (Aged 14)

Lows and highs
Oceans of emotions
Victims of the
Everlasting
No: 583   By: Dani Gatcum   (Aged 12)

Love is like a square,
Sharp edges,
Long lines,
Yet corners we have to turn.
No: 584   By: Naomi Tucker   (Aged 13)

Burning, burning
How my stomach is churning,
Yearning, yearning
Now I'm learning
No: 585   By: Beth Standing   (Aged 13)

The grass grows green and the plants grow high,
The farmer is keen and knows they won't die,
He loves his plants and cares a lot,
For now he's old they are all he's got.
No: 586   By: Beth Markwell   (Aged 13)

What is this thing called Love,
Where so many people are left behind?
Any why is love so easy to lose,
And yet, so hard to find?
No: 587   By: Ella Waddington   (Aged 13)

Like a bolt from the blue love strikes
Burning within like a flame
Some love is never extinguished
No: 588   By: Robyn Pinchen   (Class 8DA)

(Saving You) I turn away to save you
I stopped to save you
I walked away to save you
from my love
No: 589   By: Alexandra Guy   (Aged 12)

Love is like an angry flame,
Scalding you in its power,
But like a flame it always dies,
It's like an inferno you, have to control it.
No: 590   By: Patrick Powell   (Aged 13)

Love is like a storm
It blows straight through the cracks.
When you try to stop it.
The cracks grow bigger.
No: 591   By: William Gardner   (Aged 13)

(What is love?) Love? What is love?
You can't buy it in shops,
Or go looking for it in the park
You have to wait for it to come to you.
No: 592   By: Lydia O'Callaghan   (Aged 13)

Raindrops glistening on rose petals and daises
Green shoots rising above the damp spring earth
Birds chirping happily in the morning sunshine
I love this gorgeous picture of spring…
No: 593   By: Christina Rowlands   (Aged 12)

(My Grandad) I have loved, and always will love,
But now I only have a tragic memory,
Of his warm smile, crumpled skin,
And most of all, his love for life.
No: 594   By: Eliza Austin-Hall   (Aged 13)

I love basketball, the bouncing, the sound, the skill,
The passing of an orange ball,
hitting the floor, over and over,
go for a shot, suspense, it skims the rim, it's in!
No: 595   By: Robin Lewis   (Aged 13)

Taekwon-do is a martial art
It makes you work, right down to the heart
Adrenaline rushing, making me sweat,
Anyone attacks me, I'll be a serious threat!
No: 596   By: Will Hine   (Aged 13)

(Love) You can't see it
You can't catch it
You can't touch it
Love is like a silent night
No: 597   By: Tessa Young   (Aged 12)

What is love? Why is it here?
What makes the most powerful force?
It can make people do terrible or great things.
So it begs the question; who is in charge, us or the love?
No: 598   By: David Walker   (Aged 12)

(Love) Love is like a dove
You can't catch it
Even when you do catch it
It just flies away
No: 599   By: Natasha Whiddon   (Aged 15)

(My Dog) My little soft and gentle dog Sky
I love her up to the moon and back
I call her my puppy,
When she runs around and around.
No: 600   By: June Baxter   (Aged 12)

(Love Trees) twisting turning branches
a home for all wildlife
a place for kids to come and invade
the twisting turning branches of the tree
No: 601   By: Lucy Palmer   (Aged 12)

The view off the tor is spectacular, the bikers flying
Through the air as they race down the course.
Mud sprays as a golfer's golfball hits the puddle.
Tourists drive off as they think they saw the Bodmin Beast.
No: 602   By: Ollie Baker   (Aged 12)

(Love of the Sea)The shinning sun reflects onto the sparkly water.
In the sea the fish are darting through the sea
like racing cars
colourful fish look like rainbows in the upside down sea.
No: 603   By: Michael Fisher   (Aged 13)

The smell of the morning cold and wet.
Hearing all the dogs we met.
The sun bursting through the trees.
I love the feel of the morning breeze!
No: 604   By: Will Hall   (Aged 13)

Extracted purity, maturity. Faith of the earth a glint of nature,
Eager to burst and show its power, a twilight reflection
Of the moon at night. A diamond sets your heart alight
With all its power – a wonderful sight.
No: 605   By: Sally Allison   (Aged 13)

the amazing sunset on the Deep Blue Sea
the Beautiful colours clash with each other reflecting on
the water it's a breathtaking experience the warmth of
the sun fades further and further away.
No: 606   By: Sam Cooper   (Aged 12)

(The Snow Leopard) sneaky, Scary, Spooky
like a ghost the snow leopard moves
agile, smooth not a Sound on the ground,
but it's ready to pounce
No: 607   By: James Woods   (Aged 13)

I love the way dolphins jump out of the water,
They look so elegant and so peaceful,
When they swim gracefully underwater they get ready to pounce
I just love the way dolphins Play!
No: 608   By: Mathew Davidson   (Aged 12)

Enchanting scenery, fragranced breeze
Air so tender, sharp and sweet
Views too beautiful and breath-taking to speak
The breeze brings rain, which I now embrace.
No: 609   By: Natasha Barrett   (Aged 13)

There are lots of lovely things about Nature
What I love the most are the flowers
Bluebells, Roses, Snowdrops, tulips, daisy, daffodils
I love flowers the most because they make me happy.
No: 610   By: Emma Cole   (Aged 12)

Nature is beautiful
As the trees are swaying in the wind,
And the monkeys are swaying from branch to branch,
I LOVE NATURE !!
No: 611   By: Stephanie Credicott   (Aged 12)

The sun is sunny
It shines all day long
the sun makes me happy
So sing a bug song
No: 612   By: Kayleigh Edwards

Roaring rivers with the sun
Reflecting on top of the flowing
River, and the water rushing and
Crashing in and out of the ROCKS!
No: 613   By: Amy Ruth Bayliss   (Aged 12)

The Sea is like a Silent Snail Crawling and gliding
But other times it can roar like a tiger, or
Pounce like a lion
Diving in the water
No: 614   By: Abby Emberton   (Aged 13)

The Trees swooping in the wind
and the birds tweeting like mice
and the grass swaying like a dancer
and the water jumping of rocks like a grasshopper
No: 615   By: Mathew Bragg

(Family Love) I love my mum I love my dad
I love my family
Even though they make me mad
I love my family
No: 616   By: Faye Wakley   (Aged 12)

On this sunny day,
Our love shines out a ray.
Look up at the blue sky
The love of us will never die.
No: 617 A   By: Elliot Blatchford   (Aged 12)

Love is a beautiful torch,
with hugs and kisses of glee.
The happiest things of all,
We all will once see.
No: 617 B   By: Elliot Blatchford   (Aged 12)

(Loves Strength) Love is a universal bond
You can't break it its forever strong
You can't avoid it
It can be round the next corner
No: 618   By: Theo Evans

(You Are Everything) Love can mean the world to you
Every time I see you it's like a glowing star
Love is so special and deep
Love means everything
No: 619   By: Laura Taverner   (Aged 13)

Love is when two hearts correspond with each other.
Never falling from each other.
It gives light to your other.
Love, you'll always be with each other.
No: 620   By: Tom Stoneham   (Aged 13)

My Dad means the world to me!
he Loves me forever like the life of a tree
though we hardly see each other
our Love remains in our hearts
No: 621   By: Lauren Martin   (Aged 13)

(My Budgie Wally) My little puff ball, Wally,
I love him down to the ground,
We call him mini spitfire,
when he flies round and round.
No: 622   By: Lily Fitzsimmons   (Aged 12)

I adore my book,
The tales it tells,
the places it's been,
I adore reading.
No: 623   By: Jocelyn Mennell   (Aged 12)

I love my 2 very cute hamsters, Stripe and Kate,
And they stay up, very, very late,
They sometimes bite my finger, it doesn't hurt,
They like to muck around in the dirt.
No: 624   By: Laura Westacott

I love my mum so much,
She gives me kisses and hugs,
When I need it most,
She is always loving and caring
No: 625   By: Laura Westacott

I love my dad, very, very much,
He's always there when I need him,
He always sorts all my problems at school,
He is always there for me all day.
No: 626   By: Laura Westacott   (Aged 12)

(Puddles) The splash of a puddle,
The flop of a wellie,
The thud of the foot, and most of all
Peoples screams when it runs down their legs!
No: 627   By: George Conybeare   (Aged 12)

(Aunty Mary) I can remember my Aunty Mary
I was so fond of her,
She so pretty in her younger days,
But still I love her even though she's gone.
No: 628   By: Tierney Dower   (Aged 12)

I love computer games. The zip of the laser gun,
The swoosh of the spaceship
The sizzle of the aliens face
Computer games are great – level completed.
No: 629   By: George Conybeare   (Aged 12)

Love is a silly thing it gives you butterflies
It makes you lose your voice
And puts you in another planet
But we all know it is essential.
No: 630   By: George Conybeare   (Aged 12)

(Family) My family mean the world to me,
All of them are caring
Me B my sister sharing
I love my family
No: 631   By: Tierney Dower   (Aged 12)

(My Boyfriend) He makes me laugh when I am feeling down,
Sometimes we argue, which makes me frown.
This is my fairytale. Mother says it won't last.
She's wrong. He won't be a part of my past.
No: 632   By: Tabitha Crabtree   (Aged 15)

I kiss her soft pink nose
I groom her glossy coat
I tell her all my secrets
I love Spot
No: 633   By: Rebecca Tunnicliffe   (Aged 12)

(Cats) I love the way they purr
With a sparkle on their nose
I love their silky fur
It's smell like a fresh rose
No: 634   By: Luke Bailey   (Aged 13)

(Love of Dartmoor) Breeze, cold wind snaps at the gauze
The trodden grass where animals stroll
The sun gleaming from the top of the tor
The clouds crying in anger at the roaring sun
No: 635   By: George Fitzsimons   (Aged 12)

God's greatest gifts to us: life and love
Our lives need love
Let us love to live
Let's all live to love.
No: 636   By: Tony Dunk   From: Tavistock

I don't love life in France where people
have a 'Plat du Jour' nor in Germany where
they choose a 'Teller des Tages'. I love it here
where 'Today's Special – EVERY DAY'S SPECIAL'
No: 637   By: Jean Tarry, Editor- NEVER BURY POETRY

Bring to me the seashore, let me behold the waves.
Face me to salty windward that I may live again.
Let me breathe the surging ozone, watch white horses prance
To recall vast oceans and give past times a glance
No: 638   By: M.V. Ullathorne   From: Yelverton

I've worshipped the ground where you have walked,
Adored the music of your voice when we've talked,
Our love is still strong though the years roll on by,
I accept the Lord's gift and have never asked why.
No: 639   By: M.V. Ullathorne   From: Yelverton

There's gorse and there is heather, yellow and mauve together,
There are tors and spongy bog, sunshine, rain, swirling fog.
There's beauty; and the beast, for eyes a special feast,
Locations rich and regions poor; this glorious place Dartmoor.
No: 640   By: M.V. Ullathorne   From: Yelverton

(Refugees) Butterflies cram their living into a day, reminding me
of that game we played: an imaginary suitcase,
one hour to pack. The indecision of what to take,
when no possessions could guarantee survival.
No: 641   By: Julie Mellor   From: Sheffield

(Grave) Her headstone casts triangles
of shade, all sharp points
and angles:
such is the geometry of grief.
No: 642   By: Julie Mellor   From: Sheffield

(Alchemy) As the sun sets, the apple tree's leaves
turn to silver; an experiment
that can be repeated any clear evening
from April to September.
No: 643 By: Julie Mellor From: Sheffield

(Love) Its deceptions are such
that we shun the blindfold
yet insist on undressing
in the dark.
No: 644 By: Julie Mellor From: Sheffield

(Between Edington and Braton) It's a church music festival, so not
The place they'd sing 'Sure on this shinning night.
But we walked there, late summer night, in health,
And felt the starlit landscape to the north.
No: 645 By: Aidan Baker From: Cambridge

(A CYCLE) Our first bike tour was first for firstness, yes,
the new itself still new, new day new place.
Today, newness is less, firstness is full.
Yet the wheels no less strengthen in their pull.
No: 646 By: Aidan Baker From: Cambridge

(ONE TYPE OF LOVE) An arm around her shoulders
and letting her cry.
Ah, that's not what I meant,
by a holding reply.
No: 647 By: Aidan Baker From: Cambridge

(SELF-LOVE) I'M SPECAIL VEXES, without meaning to,
the special rage of I'M AS GOOD AS YOU.
--Why don't you try I'M OK YOU'RE OK?
--Yes, but it never seems to stick that way.
No: 648   By: Aidan Baker   From: Cambridge

(For Mother) You sit beside me, your still sharp-eyes admiring
carvings and stained glass, and say you're pleased we came
here. I watch the light seeking
your small face, making it younger; the worry lines erased.
No: 649 By: Josie Turner   From: Hitchin

(Renewal V1) A sunset on the Firth is joy defined,
The Isle of Arran, Ailsa Craig, Kintyre,
Each silhouette of mountain, hill outlined
In evening glow of luminescent fire.
No: 650   By: Muriel Cuttler   From: Tavistock

(V2) A silken sheen of causeway stretches wide
Across the sea, its gilded waves unfold,
Buoying the eiders on a surge of tide,
Rippling to shore in serried ranks of gold.
No: 651   By: Muriel Cuttler   From: Tavistock

(V3) In emerald flash, horizon, sun unite,
Brilliance of cloud pales over pewter gray,
Yet ebbing colour still affords delight,
No sadness, no regret at dying day.
No: 652   By: Muriel Cuttler   From: Tavistock

(V4) In every sunset early promise lies,
Creation's wonders still remain
Renewal in eternity's sunrise
When morning's glow returns again.
No: 653   By: Muriel Cuttler   From: Tavistock

(If music be the food of love…) Masses, Anthems, hymns and Psalms,
Wesley, Stanford, Bach and Brahms,
Fortify us all our days,
A never-ending Song of Praise.
No: 654 By: Mary Hawkins From: Buckland Monachorum

(The love of singing in church) When music soars,
My spirit soars
And dances with the angels
On the high, vaulted roof.
No: 655 By: Mary Hawkins From: Buckland Monachorum

(My tongue shall never tire of charting with the choir) There is a choir man named Sean
Who makes us sing from dusk to dawn,
But through our love of what we sing
The span of time means not a thing.
No: 656 By: Mary Hawkins From: Buckland Monachorum

(The Journey) So sweet is love, so cruel is pain!)
We suffer both in equal measure.
We tread the path from earth to heaven
With memories to treasure.
No: 657   By: G.M. Sanders   From: Brentor

(Love of Life) a love of life is what I have.
A life of love to you I give
Virtues of love and truth and grace
I see them all in your dear face.
No: 658   By: G.M. Sanders   From: Brentor

Love colours my life,
A multi-hued pallet of possibilities
Highlighting and shading the canvas,
unfurling life's rich tapestry.
No: 659 By: Jane Neeman (DIY Poets) From: Horrabridge

Look for it
Offer it
Value it
Enjoy it
No: 660   By: Joan Stewart   From: Tavistock

(Cliché'd Love) Love is blind, So how were roses red,
When our eyes met across a crowded room?
I'll love you forever and a day, you said.
Lead me up the garden path –we'll be wed next June!
No: 661   By: Greta Thomas   From: Tavistock

(Love) It's your heart swelling when a loved one smiles,
that fear in your stomach, when it's their time.
It touches our lives, it makes who we are,
It's a glorious moment, like a shining star.
No: 662 By: Justine Machin From: Preston, Lancashire

I love 'Bella Pelsoi', a feline so supreme
Both intelligent and beautiful and more than she may seem –
A complicated creature, a furry work of art-
Bella Pelosi, you can open the cat-flap to my heart!
No: 663   By: Mrs Paulette Pelosi   From: Swansea

I'm a Welsh-Italian, look into my brown eyes
Down into my soul, where my true love lies,
My heart resides in Italy with ancestors' spirits' strength,
Bound with chords of blood-ties, in centuries of length.
No: 664   By: Mrs Paulette Pelosi   From: Swansea

My love is more than a red, red rose
It's everything that's red!
Am I in love with this colour?
You may take that fact as read!
No: 665   By: Mrs Paulette Pelosi   From: Swansea

(This Life) We are all in this life together
and I think it is both appertain and appropriate
that I contribute my loving pratfalls
to the phantasmagorical fun of the universal circus
No: 666   By: Crispin Williams   From: St. Ives

(Love) If you are not prepared for pain,
An aching heart, a troubled brain,
To give and not to count the cost,
Love's meaningless and you'll be lost.
**No: 667   By: James Leonard-Williams   From:
Casablanca, Morocco**

I love the wind, the rain as it blows against my face,
I love the sun beating on the desert sand,
I love snow as it falls on the Scottish high land,
I love the weather because it is beyond our control.
No: 668   By: AC   From: Tavistock

(It was a step pull) up to the crest, and then I saw-all suddenly
spread out like a feast below-small vineyards,
feathered larch, a thread of river, light
on long grass waves, scudding.
No: 669   By: Margaret Wilmot   From: Selmston

(Sculpture studio: August) I got back late, and what a shock
the studio not dark, or empty after all: in a cascading funnel
of yellow light a bony man clad only in orange underpants
stood, singularly alone.
No: 670   By: Margaret Wilmot   From: Selmston

Our organists both have one thing in common,
Both Sean and Maurice share a passion,
They love to sit perched on their wooden bench,
And pull out all the stops to celebrate any noteworthy
occasion.
No: 671   By: A. Key   From: Tavistock

(In the world) An old childhood glee rose,
powerful as the smell of kelp, as I ran
alone down steps to the twilit cove, to the slap
and skelp of waves on sand.
No: 672   By: Margaret Wilmot   From: Selmston

How different from that other world, this Sainted Haven!
These mountains, forests, caves, these lulling streams
Spared from legend hatreds of dove and raven!
Not known to hide-and-seek of siren screams!
No: 673   By: Solomon Odeleye   From: London

Hands together, head bowed
On our knees we pray;
Loving Lord, glory to thee
This and every day.
No: 674   By: Mrs Aileen SB Lobban   From: Edinburgh

How blessed are we to live our lives
Full of gifts showered from above;
With circles of friends and children's smiles
'Midst laughter, music joy and love.
No: 675   By: Mrs Aileen SB Lobban   From: Edinburgh

Take a walk with me down this city's streets
Listen to the rhythm of its urban beat;
Dance to the pulse within its living heart
Love to the music and sing out your part.
No: 676   By: Mrs Aileen SB Lobban   From: Edinburgh

I send you dates,
You send me scarves and calendars,
They are a token of years of friendship, love and loyalty,
Between Christian and Muslim.
No: 677   By: Re   From: Algeria

A
cup
of
tea
No: 678   By: Jean Symons   From: Horrabridge

Dusk and the branch trembles
With the weight of speckled chickens.
A green star, high in a branch,
Some stones are still warm.
No: 679   By: Jean Symons   From: Horrabridge

Isambard Kingdom Brunel
has a name fits his fame very well,
say it out plain sounds like a train;
IS am bard KING dom bru NEL.
No: 680   By: Jean Symons   From: Horrabridge

A room, books on the floor
piled papers
entice …
Outside, rain.
No: 681   By: Jean Symons   From: Horrabridge

Roger the watch
is more a town clock than a watch,
he towers over the market,
All the traders remark it.
No: 682   By: Jean Symons   From: Horrabridge

a cup of tea
a nice cup of tea
a nice hot cup of tea
a nice hot sweet cup of tea
No: 683   By: Jean Symons   From: Horrabridge

cup of tea
with two sugars
cup of tea
with two sugars
No: 684   By: Jean Symons   From: Horrabridge

mug of tea, mug of tea
Bob always greets me,
and the teaspoon and the mug
chorus stirringly.
No: 685   By: Jean Symons   From: Horrabridge

A museum's foyer shop
And crowds and cameras,
Obscure the laborious stairs
To the mind's well-stored lairs
No: 686   By: Jean Symons   From: Horrabridge

huge-deluge river rise gives a gurt-spurt splosh
a rejoice-voice noise of delux-flux wash
surge-regurging splurge, stout-spout-shout splish splash
spray-hurray! Whirl-twirl-swirl, impact-cataract crash
No: 687   By: Jean Symons   From: Horrabridge

Love can be light
Love can be fun,
Love can be sprinkled with delight,
Just like a frothy coffee.
No: 688   By: AC   From: Tavistock

Love is like a tomato,
Sometimes it is sharp and sometimes sweet to taste,
The rich red colour is always attractive at first sight,
But then so is love!
No: 689   By: AC From: Tavistock

the telly,
is a bit like the lottery;
fine to look forward to in the rain,
but always a 'chance to see again'
No: 690   By: Jean Symons   From: Horrabridge

Love isn't easy,
It opens you up to being hurt,
Feeling pain,
But without it the world just wouldn't be the same.
No: 691   By: AC   From: Tavistock

red berry, a radish,
the human heart,
ten painted toenails,
February sun.
No: 692   By: Jean Symons   From: Horrabridge

On a chilly winter night,
The only remedy,
Is a really big hug,
From someone you cherish
No: 693　By: GC　From: Tavistock

(Swansong V1) Unison mirrowed neath a summer sky,
a stately cob, his graceful pen beside,
proud breast the waters of a gentle Wye,
together in dignity they glide,
No: 694　By: Muriel Cuttler　From: Tavistock

(V2) Between the banks of river sedge,
their partnership a constancy
of natural law, not token pledge,
unbreakable fidelity.
No: 695　By: Muriel Cuttler　From: Tavistock

(V3) Flurry of water, spread of feathered snow,
and two swans eager rise as one,
companionship of wingbeat slow,
their flight steep arrowed toward the sun.
No: 696　By: Muriel Cuttler　From: Tavistock

(V4) Your name, a whisper on my breath,
with aching heart, I watch them pass,
unsullied by the touch of death,
my tears fast falling on the meadow grass.
No: 697　By: Muriel Cuttler　From: Tavistock

(Love Prayers) Lord God, my prayer to you
each day is – Thank You
for being You, loving
Father, son and Holy Spirit.
No: 698   By: Alan Cuttler   From: Tavistock

Loving god, my thanks always
To you, for creating and
sustaining me, my family,
friends and all Creation
No: 699   By: Alan Cuttler   From: Tavistock

Loving God, as Jesus succoured
others, be with us as we
comfort others with His
boundless love and compassion.
No: 700   By: Alan Cuttler   From: Tavistock

"And God saw that it was good",
bless us and lovingly help to
work with you to restore your
Creation as you meant it to be.
No: 701   By: Alan Cuttler   From: Tavistock

(Dartmoor, Larkrise) Silence of winter moor-splinters-in a skylark's song,
rising from weave of bracken, the songster calls in exultation,
then hovers over slumberladen tors, eagerly waiting for
signs of Spring awakening, in the earth shod landscape.
No: 702   By: Muriel Cuttler   From: Tavistock

(Love) the wonder of the creation.
To have Christ as our foundation.
The hope of our Salvation.
This is everlasting love.
No: 703   By: Jean Vousden   From: Tavistock

Your exuberant generosity in painting the sky with liquid light;
The unnecessary frivolity of puffins and giraffes; your microscopic
care for detail shown in diatoms; the songs of the whale
and the ant: Facets of Your love for the world.
No: 704   By: Mrs Patsy Robinson   From: Petersfield, Hants

(Grandma) Without your passing, I knew not of what is lost,
The pain that cuts through me, razor edged, is healing balm
fluid,
My tears like willow sap, silver rinsed, in moon-light,
Fall on my cheeks, crystallising, like diamond-crust of icy
frost.
No: 705   By: Caitlin Robbins (Aged 13)   From: East Twickenham

I love cats
I love dogs
I love rabbits
and I love frogs
No: 706   By: Lily Walke (Aged 4)   From: Tavistock

Starlight,
Moonbright,
Holding hands,
Walking by the sea
No: 707   By: Anon   From: Topsham

ham, eggs and chips
porkchops, chips and peas
plaice, chips and peas
steak, chips and peas
No: 708   By: Jean Symons   From: Horrabridge

(The Seamless Garment) To have been born under such a bright star
His life was a bruised radiance. Darkness came too soon, like
night's black shadow – a seamless garment of hatred,
so sharp it made the thorns' caress a welcoming embrace.
No: 709   By: Sandra McQueen   From: Dundee

Snowdrops shone when you said yes, roses when we wed;
Through years and years loves transforms,
Though, year on year, snowdrops and roses
Shine as then.
No: 710   (Snowdrops) By: Tim Jones   From: Tavistock

Poems from St Peter's School - Tavistock

(Love) Love takes time to come
But many things you'll love,
Pets, food, family and friends,
What do you love most?
No: 711   Hannah Greep   (Aged 11)

(Love)Love is soft and gentle,
It's like a red rose, when you smell, it is sweet,
It's always with us, eventhough sometimes we don't think it is,
Love is strong and powerful.
No: 712   Amy Collacott   (Aged 11)

(Dragons) Dragons fiery breath soaring wings of flame
Great gold wings higher than high on a throne of wind
Slashing claws of pure heat melting even diamand
Dragon Scales harder than Stronger that Stron unpierceable to anything.
No: 713   Harry Nicholls   (Aged 11)

I love Football
Football rocks
I love football
all day long
No: 714   Oliver

Love is up in the sky for my Mum
and my dad and my dogs and my Cats
Love feel Happy for me and my Mum
I like it so much for my Mum
No: 715   Harry Cole   (Aged 7)

(Love) I love chocolate Yes I do,
I love chocolate how about you,
Eat some chocolate it's so yummy,
Now the chocolate's in my tummy.
No: 716   Emma Nicholls   (Aged 11)

Love can be big,
Love can be small,
Whatever the size
Make the most of it all.
No: 717   Nathan Turnock   (Aged 11)

(Love) Love is a magical word,
It brings joy to the world,
It brings people together, like a
bird to its feather.
No: 718   Kris Chapman   (Aged 11)

(Treacle my big, fat, lazy cat!)A fat bundle of ginger spotted fur,
A yellow eye blinks lazily,
You may be wondering what on earth
Could cause my cat to be so blooming lazy!
No: 719   Holly Gibbs   (Aged 11)

(Love) Love is a part of life
Open gifts from Secret people
Vilet flowers are in poems
Everyone opens there heart!
No: 720   Hannah Cox   (Aged 11)

Little ball of fluff
As black as black as coal
Travelled here with Santa
Across the white washed snow
No: 721   Nichols Piper   (Aged 10)

(Love) The petal is growing
The birds are singing
Parents are loving
and bells are dinging
No: 722   Nathan   (Aged 10)

(Love poem) On this day hearts grow
On this day people grow
On this day everyone comes together
On this day
No: 723   Zara Bartlett   (Aged 11)

(Love) Love is a beauty,
A way of life,
Love can be food,
Or your husband or wife.
No: 724   Beryl   (Aged 11)

Love means life,
Open your heart,
Valentine's day is comeing,
Everyone will celebrate.
No: 725   Kerry Watkins

I love my dog than you Lord.
I love my famle thank you Lord.
I love my friend thank you Lord.
Thank you Lord for love.
No: 726   Ethan Turner   (Aged 8)

Love is the most wonderful thing.
Love feels magic, love feels great.
There will be no happiness without love.
Love is the very best.
No: 727   Jack Mathews   (Aged 7)

Love is red.
Love is blue and so are you.
Love is white pink and blue.
Love is wonderful don't you think so too.
No: 728   Joanna Bulley   (Aged 7)

(Love Love Love Love!) Love feels good in your heart.
Love is around you.
I love my dog blue.
I love my great Gandad's medals.
No: 729   Mark Lewis   (Aged 7)

I love my dog and my cat
They make me very happy
I hug them
I like to stroke them.
No: 730   Aaron Fry   (Aged 8)

I love my dog because it gives me comfort.
When I sit down my dog sits next to me.
She puts he paw on me when she wants smoothing.
I hug my dog lots.
No: 731   Callum Rule   (Aged 7)

(I love my cat) I love my cat fluffy a sweet.
I love my cat ready to eat.
I love my cat sat upon a wall.
I love my cat ready to fall.
No: 732   Ashling Heneghan

(A love poem) I love my family
Love is like magic
Love is in heaven
I love Man utd they are the best.
No: 733   Harry Herdman

Love is Magic
Love is powerful
Love is Strong
I love love!
No: 734   Holly Kellock   (Aged 8)

(A love poem) He will be coming with love.
The greatest Lord will be coming with love.
Love is beginning to get to me.
Love is powerful, Magic the greatest thing in the world!
No: 735   Francesca Herdman   (Aged 7)

I love friends
I love mum
I love dad
I love brother
No: 736   Sam Roberts   (Aged 8)

(Love) Love is here for ever.
Love is magic as can be
who love love? we do.
love love glorious love
No: 737   Hannah Davenport   (Aged 7)

(Pets) Love pets so snug
make me so happy.
I love pets love pets so happy
I love Animals lots
No: 738   Tara Soper   (Aged 7)

(All about Love) We love love it is grat like a shooting star.
Like we love Jesus because he look after us.
Jesus love us when we were born
The whole world love Jesus
No: 739   Livvy Carr   (Aged 7)

Love is magic.
Love is brilliant.
Love is a hug from mum and dad.
Love is everywhere!
No: 740   Ben Evans   (Aged 8)

Love is the best fing in the wold.
Love is the best because it is good.
Above the wold god Give's us love.
Love is like a baid singing and the stars.
No: 741   Aimee Tolley   (Aged 7)

I love my mum and dad.
I love you.
Love is powerful
Love is magic.
No: 742   Karl Ellicott   (Aged 7)

I love my guinea pig
It is lovely like a teddy bear.
It is colourful like a sugar plum.
I love it to pieces.
No: 743   Joe D   (Aged 7)

I love my cat and
my mum and dad and
my sisters and my friends
and it is like a star.
No: 744   Lewes Hames   (Aged 7)

When she first walked in I fell in Love instantley
I offered her a rose but she backed away fast.
She ran out of the building I followed her out
I chased her she got away quickly.
No: 745   By: Jacob Hoare   (Aged 10)

(Love) Love, Love is a verb Love is a doing word.
Shakes me makes me brighter makes me Love you
Love, Love makes my life love makes me nicer.
Love Love is a verb love is a doing word
No: 746   By: Jack Rawlings   (Aged 9)

(My dog) my dog ful of Joy full of love
comes to great you when you get in
comes and meets you when you're new
If she does not know you she goes crazy
No: 747   By: Alex Frances   (Aged 9)

(Love) The 14th of february is nearly here
The day of loving and care
Valintins Day is near
Everybodys dreaming with love in the air.
No: 748   By: Emma Greening   (Aged 10)

Love is like a red red rose.
Sometimes it wilts in the cold wind that blows.
But watch out because if you think,
You will lose you love in half a blink
No: 749   By: Grainné Fitzgerald   (Aged 9)

(My poem about my dog) My dog makes me happy my dog makes me pure.
Love is pure love is great. I love my dog.
my dog cares for me and I care for him.
Love is pure love is great I love my dog. And that is great!!
No: 750   By: Alex Williams   (Aged 10)

Love is cute and lovely, It makes you smile, it loves you heart,
Take the chance it makes you bright,
you turn red and go to church and you
have a love as sweet as you.
No: 751   By: Bethany Alford   (Aged 9)

Orange and White fur Shining in the bright, Strong Sun
green glowing eyes flashing in the darkness
the highest tail of all the rest
the most beautiful of all
No: 752   By: Rory E.   (Aged 10)

My favourite month of
the year is near the
time of love and care.
Love is like a big red rose which shimers in the air.
No: 753   By: Martha Walke   (Aged 9)

I love my cat and she loves me so much. She has a furry
coat that I love stroking every mints. But she loves
chacing are rabbit over the gardon allways.
are love is like a brik wall that dosen't breack down.
No: 754   By: Lucy Miller   (Aged 9)

(My Dog Holly) My love for you is like a rose
I bet your heart sank for you're the one I chose
My love for sweet little you
is above the heavens dove
No: 755   By: Jessica Lillicrap   (Aged 9)

Love is a graceful song,
Love is a merry wrong,
Love is a crazy stare,
Love is a true life!
No: 756   By: Rachel Hooper   (Aged 10)

love is a wonderful thing
love is mostly a happy thing
love is mostly a sad thing
But love is a true thing.
No: 757   By: Beth O'Boyle   (Aged 10)

I love the wonder of my life
The cutest one for me
Love is like an angel in the sky
Like a Butterfly flying around inside.
No: 758   By: Barney Tossell   (Aged 9)

You are my blue sky of my life.
The shimmering sun
I will love you for ever.
I think you are lovely.
No: 759   By: Nathan Dodd   (Aged 10)

Dogs are so sweet golden and soft.
Cosy and warm lovely and cuddly.
Eyes glow in the pitch blackdark
Dogs are my life and I love the dearly.
No: 760   By: Joel Gilhespy   (Aged 9)

Oh, how I love the cent of roses,
Oh, how I love our lord's creation.
Oh, how I love our growing poses,
Oh, how I love your love's sensation.
No: 761   By: Angus F   (Aged 9)

Love is all around us,
We love god,
Love makes you feel like the deep blue sea,
It makes your heart rise with triumpth.
No: 762   By: Miles Pinkney   (Aged 9)

Love is all around us,
Love can be soppy,
Love is what God wanted us to do,
Love can bring people together like some glue
No: 763   By: Callum Sherrell   (Aged 9)

I love West Ham they are a good football
Team. West Ham's nicknames called the
Hammers. I love the nickname.
I love the Hammers they are the best.
No: 764   By: Joseph O.   (Aged 8)

I love my special rabbit Jake.
He makes me feel peaceful in my heart.
I love my great family.
They make me feel sweet.
No: 765   By: Megan Stone   (Aged 7)

I love my family.
They love me.
Like shimmering stars,
As lovely as can be.
No: 766   By: Marnie Hoare   (Aged 8)

Love is a piece of chocolate,
Love is a piece of your heart.
Love is a piece of everyone,
and especially yours too.
No: 767   By: Alice Egan   (Aged 7)

The things I love are the moon people and
animals and rain. Look after your environment by
puttting litter in the bin. I have a dog, cat
rabbit and hamster. I love everything.
No: 768   By: Anon

Look at the stars above and
You know you are loved by your
family and friends. With our
love it won't break.
No: 769   By: Megan Williams   (Aged 7)

Love is magic powerful and grand. I love love.
Love is when you love something or someone like a flower.
Love is precious to us xx Love mustn't hear.
Love is good and how we make friends.
No: 770   By: Anon

Love love its grand
Love is to die for
Love is a big big surprise
Love makes you happy
No: 771   By: Kurt Goman   (Aged 8)

Love is like a tree. Love is like a pea. Love is like a 3.
Love is like white and a bike. Love is like blue.
Love is like you and you and you
Do you think so too?
No: 772   By: Oscar Agnew   (Aged 8)

I love my rabbit it had a hobbit for food.
I love my guineapig it looked like a thingypig.
I love my snails because they make nice trails.
I love my dogs they like to chase frogs.
No: 773   By: Phoebe Woodhouse   (Aged 8)

Love your family
Love your friends
Love your pets
and love god
No: 774   By: Daniel Hay   (Aged 10)

Love is like a flower,
That sways in the wind,
With bees buzzing round it,
Or a lily floating on the water.
No: 775   By: Rebekah Hainsworth   (Aged 10)

Love is the beach when the waves hit the sea
She loves me she loves me not
Love is when you get something special
he loves me he loves me not.
No: 776   By: Millie Hames   (Aged 10)

I love my family and friends,
The lovely letters the girlfriends send,
The boys send letters back,
I have a girlfriend but I can't tell that.
No: 777   By: Jacob Earley   (Aged 10)

Love shines as the midnight sky,
Looks down on us when people die.
I think of my one so true love,
As the birds in the sky look like a dove.
No: 778   By: Tom Calvert   (Aged 10)

Love is forever love is true you could stay together
Love is like gold to stay in our hearts forever
When love is gone your hearts float down like paper
When your heart starts to rise it builds a wall.
No: 779   By: Lucy Higgs   (Aged 10)

I love the beaches as the sun shines in the light,
the hot sand as the hot boils through your body,
the sea light shines in your eyes can't see,
I love playing in the sand and in the sea.
No: 780   By: Katelyn Dawe   (Aged 10)

Friends count to me,
Friends count to others
Friends are a kind of
Love!
No: 781   By: Martin Montague   (Aged 11)

I love to play golf and football everyday
I started going out with someone yesterday
We play and play all day
That's something you don't see everyday
No: 782   By: Lewis Brereton   (Aged 10)

Love is when you are with your family.
Love is when you are with friends
Love is when you are with pets or possessions
Love is all around us.
No: 783   By: James Bartlett   (Aged 10)

Love is a bird that flies off its branches
and feelings are the leaves on its twigs
happiness and heartbreak are the fruit beside the leaves
The love tree is a tree of magic things close to god
No: 784   By: Cassian Bennett   (Aged 10)

Love is romance,
Happy to be with you in my life
Every day hearts pink and red
Flow around with me and you.
No: 785   By: Jasmine Bartlet   (Aged 10)

Love can be yours,
Yes it is everywhere,
Just wait and be patient,
then your time will come
No: 786   By: Kimberly Upcott   (Aged 10)

Love cats, love dogs, love pets.
Love mum, love dad, love family.
Love cricket, love tennis, love sports.
Love English, love maths, love lessons.
No: 787   By: Ben Hosking   (Aged 10)

Love is red, pink, white and blue,
Love is love hearts, roses and sweets,
Love is flowers, cards and all kisses.
Love is the 14th of February!
No: 788   By: Ben Steel   (Aged 10)

Love is all around us, it can also be anything
Love is being with friends and family and caring.
I love my parents and pets and help my friends.
Love is full of happiness, adoring and sharing and kind.
No: 789   By: Shanelle Bowyer   (Aged 10)

Beaches are beautiful
Berries are sweet
You are all of these
But you are also my treat.
No: 790   By: James   (Aged 10)

I love the warm summer afternoons,
Staying up late and having water fights.
I love those cold winter nights,
Sitting by the fire and drinking cocoa.
No: 791   By: Joseph Wheeler   (Aged 10)

Summer summer,
I love the summer with the shining daffodils
Summer summer
I love the summer with the shining sun
No: 792   By: Adam D.

I love my family
I love my friends
I love rabbits
I love me little sister
No: 793   By: Anon

Love is great
Love is good
Love is beautiful
We should respect the people who love us
No: 794   By: Anon

I love my family as well as my friends too,
Like the ocean swaying with love.
I love you Lord,
As you love me too.
No: 795   By: Amy Lynch

I love my mates
I love my family
I love all the friends
They're the best friends I've ever had.
No: 796   By: Anon

Love is good, when people care,
Love is good when people share,
L.o.v.e. L.o.v.e.
Love is good when children play.
No: 797   By: J. Tolley

I Love my family,
I Love my friends,
I Love god's creashtion,
And god Loves the people evry were.
No: 798   By: Jamie Toms D.

I Love my family
They love me
I love my family
That's the way it's going to be.
No: 799   By: Emily MC

I love my family,
They are very kind,
I love my family,
They make me laugh.
No: 800   By: Anon

I love my family.
I love my brothers.
I love my sisters.
I love Mum and Dad.
No: 801   By: Jason Holland

Love is great,
Love is good,
I'll take your word that I love you and you Love me.
I'm glad I didn't leave you, but I'll leave you someday.
No: 802   By: Laura J. Fluin

I love the world,
With beautiful seasons,
I love the flowers that grow
And to see the baby lambs in the field
No: 803   By: Anon

I love the world as much as you,
Autumn, winter, summer and spring,
Thank you Lord for the world you gave us,
Thank you Lord for everything.
No: 804   By: Anon

I love my family,
Who love me.
I love my friends
And they love me.
No: 805   By: Susmi Benny

I Love my family yes I do
My family are very kind and lovely too
I've got lots of friends their happy and kind
I keep all I love in my mind.
No: 806   By: Lucy

I love my -
They help me at school
Our friendship never ends
because we love each other
No: 807   By: Anon

We open the gate to the path of Love,
Soaring magnifisantly like a dove,
Sharing the Love round and round,
Love is worth more than a million pound.
No: 808   By: Mariah Calvert

I Love my mum
and she loves me.
I Love my dad
And he loves me.
No: 809   By: Anon

I love the Autumn the golden grass
I love the Autumn the colourful leaves
I love the Autumn the breezy wind
I love the Autumn the rustling
No: 810   By: Caleb Prouse

I Love birds with their fluttering wings
the shinning sun shines its hottest when
I go to the beach,
The water sparkles like the stars,
the sand is soothed by the water.
No: 811   By: Jack Veevers

Love is the key to my life
Love is the best thing in my life,
I love my parents, my sisters,
I love all my family.
No: 812   By: Phoebe Sanders

I love my family,
Because they love me,
Because they take me on holiday
Because they care for me.
No: 813   By: Selina

Family of love, family of care,
Family of friends everywhere
Family of peace that care for their friends,
Family that listen to you.
No: 814   By: Hannah

I love all the seasons spring is when animals are born,
Summer is lovely and warm,
Autumn is when the leaves fall,
But winter is white with snow.
No: 815   By: Jonathan

Spring days I love them,
It's the time of new things,
birds and plants.
I love them all.
No: 816   By: Adam J.

I Love animals,
I Love pets,
They are really cute.
They are the greatest thing in the world.
No: 817   By: Aidan Evans

I love the sunny summer days,
That makes the world glaze,
I love the spring when flowers grow,
The sunnier it gets the more I glow
No: 818   By: Millie Cox

I love spring when all the small cuddly lambs are born.
I love it when I get to see them.
It's fun when my sister and I get to play with them.
And may we thank you god for all the lovely things.
No: 819   By: Ellen

Love is great we love our family,
Love is good we love our animals,
Love is great we love our friends,
Love is good we love our world.
No: 820A   By: Tate Budge

I love autumn days when the grass is wet.
I love autumn trees with golden leaves.
I love the tiny birds and their little wings.
And may we thank God for all these things.
No: 820B   By: Millie Steel

I Love Autumn days,
When the leaves blow on the ground,
And the sunny days,
when the sun shines on me.
No: 821   By: Caly Glover

Poetry in the Pews - 2008

The Dartmoor Pony's clip, clop and clatter,
Everywhere I go, they smile in the wind.
The moor brightens up my face,
Thats why I love Dartmoor.
No: 822   By: Emily Prichard

If your heart is black and
you only have a dog
Just turn and look up there
to a person named god.
No: 823   By: Laurence Harrison

Love is good,
Love is hard,
Because we will get through,
We will still be friends.
No: 824   By: Imogen Hollete

We all have love
It makes us care
love is something
We always share
No: 825   By: Richard Montague

I love the spring because of its flowers
And the Autumn because of its leaves.
I love the Summer because if it's warm weather,
And the Winter because of the snow.
No: 826   By: Caitlan Chapman

I love the summer
The baking hot sun
The walk along the beach
The bright blue sky
No: 827   By: Daniel Gibbs

Love is sweet, soft and gentle,
Love can look us in the eye and we can't see it,
Love is strong and passionate,
Love we cannot live without it.
No: 828   By: Amy Collacott   (Aged 11)

(The dark side of love) Every time a petal falls,
A heart breaks.
Every time a tear is shed,
A heart shatters.
No: 829   By: Isabelle Hall   (Aged 11)

More poems from adults

Love's gossamer touch,
Gentle bonds that bind
The heart
In fragile multiplicity.
No: 830   By: Anon   From: Tavistock

like the dew, love softly falls,
Collects around the heart.
Seeps within, pervades our breath,
and is returned to fall again.
No: 831   By: Anon   From: Tavistock

Beware the jaws that bite, the claws that rend.
Love's fond embrace men's minds doth bend.
There's no escape – few try to flee
My heart is mine, but owns to thee.
No: 832   By: Anon   From: Tavistock

Like tremulous stars
Our hearts enthralled
Volunteer,
Endlessly open to love.
No: 833   By: Anon   From: Tavistock

Love can be given in a moment,
A look,
A friendly smile,
A kind and reassuring word.
No: 834   By: G. James   From: Tavistock

We met so recently yet it feels like a lifetime,
You now live in every part of my life.
Your touch thrills as though I was a lost soul
Returning from the wilderness
No: 835   By: Jim Clements-Loftus   From: Redhill

(Elidus on Scilly) This bleak ocean is no deity
though might there be goodness in it?
And I would have a power named,
such weirdness becoming our own word.
No: 836   By: Lawrence Upton   From: Sutton, Surrey

(Farewell) Young hands waving, scarves fluttering
like the white sails of boats racing
towards horizons that we know
only they will reach
No: 837   By: Gabriel Griffin   From: Orta, Italy

(Trinity) The Father is the breath before the Thought.
The Thought takes flesh and form, becomes the Word.
The Word takes wing and flies among
The peoples of the world.
No: 838   By: Gabriel Griffin   From: Orta, Italy

(Childhood) Poppies grow as children do,
slower than watching, quicker than you are aware;
their childhood a field you jump right into
and find yourself no longer here but- there.
No: 839   By: Gabriel Griffin   From: Orta, Italy

(Angel) You are painting an angel in watercolours
on a mirror, watching the colours
blur, slip, slide away, while you stare
into the mirror. At the angel.
No: 840   By: Gabriel Griffin   From: Orta, Italy

Love is free from you to me,
from me to you, don't you see.
share it with your village, town or city;
pass it on, heal the world –love universally.
No: 841   By: Marigold Rumble   From: Shaftesbury

(Homecoming) On long summer days moonset and sunrise merge.
Old friends greet me as if we never parted;
here, my heart unbreaks and I feel I've come home.
with gentle tentacles Thurso holds my heart.
No: 842   By: Bettina Jones   From: Bury

Robins singing, bravely, brightly, persisting winter to Spring, life, love
Rooks, cawing, pairing. building, building high, love,
Blackbirds pairing, alarm calls making, protecting partners, love
All things springing, gathering, growing, evidence of Spring, God, love.
No: 843   By: Margaret Godsland   From: Exeter

We love the World we live in
so treat it just like gold
No other World in which to live
Let not our love grow cold
No: 844   By: V.J.P.   From: Tavistock

Love eager, ravenous, sigh, heavenly, yearning, stab, breath, thrill, longing
Give ecstatic call lean now wonder rapture engaged desire eternal
Lover repent temptation now wistful lay yonder reflecting goal self
Fervent tantalising grows solitudes sweet threads draws West to evolve
No: 845   By: Catherine Randle   From: Andover

Only you have shown me love
Through your eyes I've seen.
That I may be have once been soaked in sin
But your love has made me white and clean
No: 846   By: Oyinda Fakeye   From: Stanmore

Love is your heart flowing
Love is your mind knowing
Love is your soul showing
God is love.
No: 847   By: M. Malens   From: Gunnislake

The distance between violets and violation
is inestimable
like gossamer strand upon which
The balance of love and disdain pivots precariously
No: 848   By: Brian Hicks   From: Tavistock

Love
Exalts
Allowing
Flight
No: 849   By: Brian Hicks   From: Tavistock

I hold your hand
You hold my heart –
I'm filled with fear
That we shall part.
No: 850   By: Christine Breckwell   From: Plymouth

Huge sugary doughnut,
On my plate,
Heaven in an instant,
But oh, the weight.
No: 851   By: Christine Breckwell   From: Plymouth

Elusive, wonderous, amazing love
always desired, often denied
but there to find
If you look hard enough
No: 852   By: Cynthia Carpenter   From: Plymouth

Roses are red
Violets are blue
Wild strawberries are sweet
And so are you
No: 853   By: Alex   From: Sweden (translated poem)

Love is such a giving thing
to some it's not expected
It should not waiver, not at all
If not reciprocated.
No: 854   By: Lorraine Olver   From: Plymouth

Look at the word which makes us strong
Or helps our world to right the wrong
Victory is promised in his name
Everymore, He remains the same
No: 855   By: Anne Everest   From: Sidmouth

May all you wish for yourself come true
and every day have some sky that's blue.
God's love will stay close by your side
Along new paths as your faithful guide.
No: 856   By: Anne Everest   From: Sidmouth

(Love) Love is the past and all we knew
Love is the present and all who care
Love is the future and the world we'll share
Love is for ever, the promise to come.
No: 857   By: Anne Everest   From: Sidmouth

Thank you dear friends for your support,
Love shines out from your every action,
Collecting poems, typing and even laminating,
Giving freely of your time, and not just to be polite!
No: 858   By: V. Thankful   From: Tavistock

I love my little dog Oscar
He is my baby boy
He is with me on my walks
And gives me lots of joy
No: 859   By: Jenny Martin   From: Tavistock

As girls we loved to ride our bikes in the park
And in those days could stay there until dark
Carefree days all summer long
Sadly now those days are gone
No: 859   By: Jenny Martin   From: Tavistock

Just after the war there were very few sweets
And I loved sugar sandwiches as a picnic treat
With a bottle of pop and a sandwich of spam
A whole day of pleasure away from me mam
No: 860   By: Jenny Martin   From: Tavistock

When I was a girl I loved to ride my Dartmoor pony
Through streams and over tors we were never lonely
Past gorse and bracken and heather
We galloped over the moors in all kinds of weather
No: 861   By: Jenny Martin   From: Tavistock

I love a raspberry jelly or strawberry if I can
For a special Sunday treat with sandwiches of ham
Followed by some fruit cake
And bread and cream and jam
No: 862   By: Jenny Martin   From: Tavistock

I love to have my friends around for a natter and a knit
We try to put the world to rights as we chatter and sit
We cover all the headlines currently in the news
And find it very interesting that we have such different views
No: 863   By: Jenny Martin   From: Tavistock

After the nighttime comes he dawn
After the darkness light
After the winter comes Spring
Bringing new delight
No: 864   By: Jenny Martin   From: Tavistock

After the shadow comes the sun
After the storm comes peace
After the loss and loneliness
Tears will surely cease
No: 865   By: Jenny Martin   From: Tavistock

My first real boyfriend was called Keith
And I remember he had very white teeth
He was the first one to give me a real kiss
And at the age of thirteen this was bliss
No: 866   By: Jenny Martin   From: Tavistock

My favourite food is junket
I could eat it all day long
I love to make it in the microwave
So I don't have to wait too long
No: 867   By: Jenny Martin   From: Tavistock

So precious is the love of a child
Loving and giving
So tender and mild
Makes life worth living
No: 868   By: Nola Venton   From: Plymouth

Chocolate is one of the loves of my life,
Another is my wife,
But offered a choice between the two,
I couldn't decide, could you?
No: 869   By: Anon   From: Tavistock

A stellar event,
Love like a shooting star,
But beware of the black holes of jealously,
That can swallow up all hopes of wedded bliss.
No: 870   By: Joan Cheikh   From: Tavistock

Writing poetry with a friend,
Exchanging laughter,
Giggling with delight,
An expression love on bleak winter nights.
No: 871   By: Joan Cheikh   From: Tavistock

(WORDS OF LOVE) My love is hard to put in words
It's difficult to tell
What my feeling's really like
Although I know it well.
No: 872   By: Jan Robinson   From: Tavistock

My love is like a poem
No reason but with rhyme
A simple rich emotion
That will last through time.
No: 873   By: Jan Robinson   From: Tavistock

My love's not a short story
There's no twist at the end
My lover, partner, helpmate
You're also my best friend.
No: 874   By: Jan Robinson   From: Tavistock

My love is like a novel
Which slowly will unfold
Fulfilling both our lives
Lasting till we're old.
No: 875   By: Jan Robinson   From: Tavistock

My love is like a library
Not just a single book
It's deep and all-encompassing
You enslave me with a look.
No: 876   By: Jan Robinson   From: Tavistock

You smile no doubt to think of me knitting for you,
But you will know when you receive my gift,
That my family and I have never forgotten shared desert nights,
For you are still our Christian sister beloved by her Muslim ones.
No: 877   By: Re   From: Algeria

(Love) Love, ubiquitous yet unknown,
Only poets seem to have its measure.
Verily, the subject makes most of us groan,
Exasperated by this fickle, yet enchanting treasure.
No: 878   By: Brian Hicks   From: Tavistock

Love, an emotion.
Love, an illusion.
Love, an abstraction.
A four letter word.
No: 879   By: Brian Hicks   From: Tavistock

Our popular young vicar is most courageous
He has hosted something new at St Eustachius
It will be the first parish church for what its worth
To contain the most poems on love on God's earth
No: 880   By: AP   From: Tavistock

Who could love the ugly mechanical grabber?
Whose job is to keep the river Tavy clear
He has spoilt our beloved view of the bridge and the river
And many of us in Tavistock pray that he will disappear
No: 881   By: AP   From: Tavistock

I am not going to write you a Valentine
It really is too gross
You know that I think you are divine
And I love you the most
No: 882   By: AP   From: Tavistock

You are my ray of sunshine
My little piece of toast
You know that you are mine
And I love you the most
No: 883   By: AP   From: Tavistock

Love is a golden treasure
Which should last for years
Gaining strength we can measure
From laughter endurance and tears
No: 884   By: AP   From: Tavistock

There are many Inuit words for snow
To convey its forms and icy whiteness
But there is only one word that I know
To express my feelings for your delightfulness
No: 885   By: AP   From: Tavistock

I love community projects
Like poetry in the pews
And with love as the subject
It will always be in the news
No: 886   By: AP   From: Tavistock

I love the evening when the light grows dim
To see reflections lengthen in the canal's still water
A peace and calm emanates from within
And at this hour I feel that I am truly Tavistock's daughter
No: 887   By: AP   From: Tavistock

I love the spring when the horse chestnut trees
Unfold their furry hand-like leaves
Closely followed by candlesticks of flowers
The joy of spring is held in those bowers
No: 888   By: AP   From: Tavistock

I love a drift of snowdrops in the spring
Before the insects are on the wing
Their sparkling white jewels lift our hearts
A proud announcement that winter is past
No: 889   By: AP   From: Tavistock

I am not a regular church goer
I do not have strong religious views
But at Christmas I love the carols
And you will find me in the pews
No: 890   By: AP   From: Tavistock

Like a mysterious disease,
An epidemic of emotion,
Love spreads its way around the everyday world,
Transforming, healing with its touch.
No: 891   By: Sarah Pendle   From: Tavistock

I have made my vows, my promises,
For better, for worse, for my lifetime.
You have given me everything,
Eternally, in your Son.
No: 892   By: Sarah Pendle   From: Tavistock

Golden, glorious, majestic and powerful,
You radiate every corner of the world,
Shining precious light into the dark stable,
Into my darkness, lighting me, for you, God.
No: 893   By: Sarah Pendle   From: Tavistock

I love words.
Reading, writing, crosswords.
I don't like cross words.
But I do love Wordsworth.
No: 894   By: EW   From: Tavistock

Pure white splits
Into a myriad of colours
the loveliness brings pure joy,
Awe and wonder. I never cease to be amazed.
No: 895   By: EW   From: Tavistock

The Unicorn, with its magnificent beauty
And ethereal appearance.
Is it mythical? Is it real?
Only love is real.
No: 896   By: EW   From: Tavistock

The Rose, petals curled,
Lovely perfume,
Melts my heart,
Especially the Peace rose.
No: 897   By: EW   From: Tavistock

The Dove, I love.
A sign of peace,
Tranquility, purity,
Everlasting love.
No: 898   By: EW   From: Tavistock

Love and marriage,
Horse and carriage,
Tandem life,
Husband and wife.
No: 899   By: EW   From: Tavistock

Love is holding hands across a room
Of people who are distanced by time
Voluntarily touching and
Energising their receptive fields
No: 900   By: Beverley Beck   From: Tavistock

Letters combined form words
Often telling a tale which is
Variable distinct with
Emotions contained, word refrained
No: 901   By: Beverley Beck   From: Tavistock

Like all words this
One also suffers abuse
Various interpretations and use
Emotive, powerful four letters infused.
No: 902   By: Beverley Beck   From: Tavistock

What you see is what you are the man in white pursed his lips
Wilson he directed his pointed barb at my chocolate sated stomach
My love she liquidated the words from her scathing mouth
They laughed the warm circle of friends finding a container for their ire.
No: 903   By: Jan Wilson   From: Horndon

I'm not a runner, but I love to run.
I'm not a dancer, but I love to dance.
I am a man, learning to love my maleness.
I live, poised on the lip of knowing my path.
No: 904   By: Andrew Forrester   From: Horndon

(How It Moves) It's good to say 'I love you,' no doubt about
That. But – a blot of coffee sunk into the page,
A wedge of colour coming up through the photo
After years- love has already spilt the beans.
No: 905   By: Richard W.Halperin   From: Paris, France

To my beloved
I love you so much my heart will go on with you.
When I kiss your lips it makes me shiver
It makes my tummy warm
No: 906   By: Angela Kuchenbeck   From: Tavistock

I loved you from the beginning
I'll love you to infinity
I'll love you utterly – I'll never change
Love from, GOD.
No: 907 By: Mrs Ros Knight From: Class 4 Teacher BM

Here then is love
Vulnerable, sacrificial, pinned to a cross.
Here then is love
Vibrant from the grave.
No: 908 By: Mrs Ros Knight From: Class 4 Teacher BM

Creative, all-embracing
Delightful, inclusive
Perfect and purifying
Known, yet unfathomable.
No: 909 By: Mrs Ros Knight From: Class 4 Teacher BM

Precious, vital
Illuminating the darkest path
Comforting the deepest sorrow,
Beautifying everyone.
No: 910 By: Mrs Ros Knight From: Class 4 Teacher BM

(V1) Love can be … Wonderful, Exciting, Challenging.
Love can make you grin like a Cheshire Cat,
Just at the thought of his name.
Love makes you open-hearted.
No: 911   By: Anon   From: Tavistock

(V2) Love can make an ordinary person feel
very special.
Love can take you out of your comfort zone
to boldly go…
No: 912   By: Anon   From: Tavistock

(V3) Love can be short-lived.
Love lost can make you utterly miserable. Distraught.
Yet even this can give you courage to trust, to talk
Love can become a friendship; a happy and sad memory.
No: 913   By: Anon   From: Tavistock

(Mobile dog Wash) It's just across the rows
Of deadly spinning wheels
Where every puppy shows
The cleanest pair of heels
No: 914 By: Seamus Harrington From: A Coastal Town

Love and generosity go hand in hand,
The pair aren't often found,
But when they are combined
they have the power to change ordinary lives
No: 915   By: GMJ   From: Tavistock

Love can creep up on you and pounce
You may not open your door to it,
But it will push its way in,
And when it has arrived your only hope is that it will stay awhile.
No: 916   By: GMJ   From: Tavistock

My mother was a loving soul,
She cared with every strand of her soul,
She fought for those less able than herself,
She was indeed a noble women.
No: 917   By: GMJ   From: Tavistock

I love my glass of sherry,
Or sometimes a sip of ginger wine,
A gin and tonic now that's a treat,
Especially with my dog curled up beside my feet.
No: 918   By: GMJ   From: Tavistock

Little N too, I love you,
you are a little treasure.
I love you with all my heart,
you bring us so much pleasure.
No: 919   (For Little N) By: Elizabeth Bennet   From: Tavistock

Poems from Lady Modiford's School - Walkhampton

I love fire,
The way it glows at night,
Flickers when the wind blows
And the way it changes colour
No 920   By: Louis Kirkpatrick   (Aged 10)

The peacocks feather as soft as cotton,
His tail waving in the wind.
His beautiful body light and colourful.
He is beautiful smooth and elegant.
No 921   By: Hugo Challis   (Aged 8)

Love is strong, big and bold,
It can be frightening for us all,
Earth has brought this gift upon us,
A treasured gift not to regret.
No 922   By: Emily Tidy   (Aged 10)

The horse as strong as a rock tensing his muscles.
I love his pure black hair his hot breath steaming.
He gallops around the field his mane in the wind
His hooves thundering along churning the grass.
No 923   By: Richard Cann   (Aged 9)

Running oh running it's the best.
Pokerman oh pokerman it's up West.
Argyle oh Argyle it's the best but if you don't
like them drive up West.
No 924   By: Jacob Kirkpatrick   (Aged 9)

I have two ferrets they are a mess
But I even let them down my vest
They sit on my shoulder and whisper in my ear
That's why I love them so much
No 925   By: Tom Eggins   (Aged 9)

I love mango it is so tasty
We can share it all together
It's glowing like a golden star
this is why I love mango
No 926   By: Ryan Brown

I love being with my pets
they will always be there for you
whenever I'm upset I talk to them
and they will squeak back
No 927   By: Carrie-Ann McDermott

I love sport I love football
I love my dogs they smell
like frogs they jump up and lick
but they don't fetch sticks
No 928   By: Lee Thyer   (Aged 10)

I love my ponies lots and lots.
I love my dogs lots and lots.
I love my chickens lots and lots,
I'll play with my pets so happy and proud
No 929   By: Alice Kodritsch

I love my hamster to the world.
If I could be a hamster too
I see my hamster curl up to me.
I love my hamster to the world.
No 930 A   By: Sophie Smale   (Aged 9)

Love is a glorious gift in life
Our world is surrounded,
Vanishing and opening up
Everyone has found it
No 930 B   By: Rebecca Steuart   (Aged 10)

Lovely food delicious food I love food
It is yummy it is scrummy I love food
Cucumber is my favourite green and circular
It is so tasty food food, lovely food!
No 931   By: Mathew Jury   (Aged 10)

I love food, food is rich sweet and nice.
Eat, eat, eat that's all I think about.
I eat till I can't eat no more.
Every second it's eat, eat, eat.
No 932   By: Elliot Lister   (Aged 9)

I love my toys I love them lots yes indeed.
I love my house I love it lots yes indeed.
I love my pets I love them lots yes indeed.
I love my room I love it lots yes indeed.
No 933   By: Daqlin Smart   (Aged 9)

Fire agate are red like magma.
Sapphires are blue like the big ocean.
Rose quartz is pink like the pinkest plant of them all.
And the Jasper is the only rock dog I know.
No: 934   By: Floyd Ogle   (Aged 11)

I've got a pet called Roddy.
I love him, I love him.
He likes to play with his toys, toys
I love him and I love him very much
No 935   By: Adam Piper   (Aged 8)

Love is a feeling,
You know when you have it
and when you lose it,
it's about gorgeousness, honesty, emotion and trust.
No 936   By: Joe Dyer   (Aged 11)

Love is in the air around you,
Our God is the maker of love,
Visual love is a form of bonding,
Everyone here has love.
No 937   By: James Anderson   (Aged 10)

Our lives are surrounded by love,
love we give to things like cats or dogs,
this love is sent from our maker above,
Who loves us forever and always
No 938   By: Tanya Wylie   (Aged 11)

Love, love is a wonderful thing,
We love our parents we love to sing.
Love, love is a fantastic thing,
We all love our family and everything.
No 939   By: India Galbraith   (Aged 9)

I love my cat I don't know why?
Lots of craziness in his little head but it's funny,
Our cat is a ball of fun he's crazy,
Very fluffy and cute but he goes to sleep a lot.
No 940   By: Nina Ives

I love hamsters, cats, dogs
Birds, tigers, lions and frogs
All of our love is in the air
because we love to share.
No 941   By: Thomas Shipp   (Aged 9)

I love to dance, I love to dance
Everywhere I go.
I love to prance, I love to prance
And that you all should know.
No 942   By: Lauren Emony   (Aged 9)

Love is an important emotion in life,
It's what makes our world forgiving and kind.
Loves in your sister, dad, mum, husband and wife,
Love belongs to everyone, always have someone in mind.
No 943   By: Tess Ashen   (Aged 11)

Love is full of enjoyment,
Happiness for all to share,
I love my cats,
as they are cute beyond compare
No 944   By: Amelia Burnard   (Aged 10)

Your love is like the golden buttercup,
As beautiful as a sunlit tiger lily,
Your scent like a scented red rose,
But my love for you is beyond compare.
No 945   By: Megan Groom   (Aged 10)

(Two great hearts) One love a true love, a person we all embrace.
Open you mind and think, a big, bold, bright face.
All it takes is two great hearts
to make the world not so dark.
No 946   By: Jake Woodgate   (Aged 10)

Loving pets or family members, is definitely not the same,
As loving a piece of furniture or latest video game.
Loving someone is easy when they are here today,
But the love for someone who's gone won't ever go away.
No 947   By: Melanie Zelinda Brown   (Aged 10)

If you had the choice, what would you do?
Sit alone, or be outside of your home?
Taking risks, having fun, on the animal I love,
The horse, Gods creation, will help you feel the love!
No 948   By: Lily Spry   (Aged 10)

I love my guitar
When I play my guitar I feel proud of myself
I enjoy it in my fingers and my head
I love music
No 949   By: Richard Young

I love playing drums because of how they make their sound,
Drums make me feel important and special,
Drums I think are beautiful when they pound,
I love drums because of the music they play.
No 950   By: Tommy Kalnins

(My Lovely Dog) You are up in heaven my lovely
and I will never forget you never ever
I need you to know I love you so
you're out there and you love me too
No 951   By: Alice Neal   (Aged 9)

Of the people in the world, there's one for me
That's my Grandad, he has the kindest soul
His heart is pure as gold and full of love
And even when he's gone, he'll still be my Grandad
No 952   By: Jade McDermott   (Aged 11)

I love my Mum and Dad because they care for me.
If I didn't have them I wouldn't feel safe.
I love my Mum, I love my Dad, I am really glad.
I feel really special the way they love me too.
No 953   By: Ryan Shirlow   (Aged 9)

Pompy is my favourite toy,
He brings me fund and joy.
Pompy gets me to my sleep
I love him, if I don't have him I weep.
No 954   By: Tom Christopher Robert Cooper   (Aged 7)

I love my dog because she's a loving, cute pup.
If I hurt myself, she'll lick me till I laugh!
She makes me feel happy, excited and bouncy.
And she loves me when I say the word 'walkies'.
No 955   By: Hannah Gordon   (Aged 11)

The snow leopard prowled in the moonlights vision,
She spotted prey, a baby deer driven from the herd.
She stalked the deer which she depended on for survival
They are truly magnificent and easily loved.
No 956   By: Callum Mankoo-Bowers   (Aged 10)

(True Love) There is always true love in the world,
All it takes is some trying to find the one,
to find the one who will care for us
All it takes is some trying
No 957   By: Callum Cunningham   (Aged 9)

I love my guinea-pig.
Martha trusts me, they let me pick them up
Snowy trusts me too
Even if I put them out
No 958   By: William Kirkpatrick   (Aged 9)

I love football it's my kind of sport
It makes me feel special
And it's my sort. My friends think
I'm excellent and I love football
No 959   By: Adam Thyer   (Aged 10)

Love for the cheetah is very strong,
Its teeth razor sharp to dig into its prey,
Its balance is immense from its tail so long,
I hope to see it one adventurous day.
No 960   By: Mikey Ives   (Aged 11)

I love art because I'm really passionate about it.
I love it because I can let out my ideas.
I love to draw people and strange creatures.
Through my drawing I feel talented.
No 961   By: Thomas Smale   (Aged 10)

When I'm riding on my pony
I sense that she is feeling proud.
I love that feeling of jumping high
It's just us two, it's not a crowd.
No 962 A   By: Lauren Jane Gregory

I love the things around me,
I love the bird song.
I love the flowing river.
And I love the summer sun.
No 962 B   By: Molly John (Aged 9)

More Children's Poems

Love means to me a lot of stuff like
Jesus and God and other people I care about like
Mum Connor Dad Jojo
My friends and my teacher
No: 963 By: Morgan Buckley (Aged 6) From: St. Rumons

Love means to me a lot of stuff like at bedtime
When I am tucked in my bed
Snuggled with the covers over me
it makes me feel happy.
No: 964 By: Morgan Buckley (Aged 6) From: St. Rumons

Love means to me a lot of stuff
like when Mum and Dad cook my dinner
it makes me feel happy
and I feel proud of Mum and Dad.
No: 965 By: Morgan Buckley (Aged 6) From: St. Rumons

I love my parents for they help and guide me.
I love my school and my friends and my teachers
I love Valentines Day for everyone can show their love.
I love most of all being fun, healthy, happy me.
No: 966 By: Shanelle Bowyer (Aged 10) From: St. Peters

Love is all around us, love is from the heart.
Love is caring, sharing, and giving when it's needed.
Love is the wonders and joys I see each day.
Love is given by Mummy, Daddy and my sisters.
No: 967 By: Bradley Bowyer (Aged 5) From: St. Rumons

(My love) I give my heart to you,
To show how much I care,
My love will grow into,
A loving teddy bear.
No: 968   By: Jennifer Adkins   From: St. Rumons

(My Granddad) I had never met my granddad but had seen photos
But he would have been the best in the world,
I heard that he was the best farmer then,
He is brought alive by the stories people have told.
No: 969   By: Victoria Heelis   From: Tavistock College

(Love is Peace) Loving People around you,
Saying thoughts in your mind,
Families singing together,
Love is peace inside.
No: 970   By: Victoria Heelis   From: Tavistock College

Love is nature,
A sea of lie with many exits,
Love is beauty like a lovely sunset
Love is a tiger hunting you down
**No: 971   By: Rebecca Eldridge (Aged12)   From:
Tavistock College**

(A Special Place) America is awesome, Paris is so pretty
Spain is spectacular, London – a great city
Africa is beautiful, as is Sydney and Rome
But the best place in the whole world has to be my HOME
**No: 972   By: Nicola Henderson (Aged 14)   From:
Moffat, Scotland**

Love is something wonderful
that can't be bought or sold
It really is more precious
than silver or of gold.
No: 973   By: Martha Walke (Aged 9)   From: Tavistock

(Nature) Nature is a little bubble that bobs
all around you, a special feeling.
You look after it, and it will
look after you.
No: 974   By: Shayahi Kathirgamanathan (Aged 8)
From: North Harrow

Yellow sunbeams
gild her cello
while notes of liquid gold
float out into the mellow air
No: 975   By: Georgina Lloyd Owen (Aged 9)   From:
London

Jelly beans and jam tarts too
I could not love anything more than you
Apple Bonbons and jam on toast
These are the things I love the most
No: 976 By: Sophie Wildman (Aged 14) From: Plymouth

They come out yellow in Spring to brighten our day
you are beautiful like them in every way
I wrote this poem so you could hear me say
Unlike them soon gone, I love you everyday
No: 977   By: Helen Radcliffe (Aged 16)   From: Stoke
Climsland

I love it more than the sun in the sky
I hate it always having to say goodbye
You hold me so close, you make me feel snug
I just love it when you give me a hug
No: 978   By: Helen Radcliffe (Aged 16)   From: Stoke
Climsland

Blood rushing through my body giving it may all
I will dance all night unti' I fall
No one can stop me doing what I think right
I will do what I love right through the night
**No: 979   By: Helen Radcliffe (Aged 16)   From: Stoke
Climsland**

They will listen to you and give you advice
In your hour of need they would not think twice
By your side they'll be until the end
To put a smile on your face an eternal friend
**No: 980   By: Helen Radcliffe (Aged 16)   From: Stoke
Climsland**

Helping them to work and play
It's not a job I love everyday
I see those children crack a smile
I hope they will stay for awhile
**No: 981   By: Helen Radcliffe (Aged 16)   From: Stoke
Climsland**

In some way everything reminds me of you
Every touch, smell and taste leave another memory
You will never leave me, however far away
There's a place in my heart for you always
**No: 982   By: Helen Radcliffe (Aged 16)   From: Stoke
Climsland**

I want you to always stay by my side
Look deep into my eyes and kiss me
When I said I hated you I lied
What we have is love, can't you see?
**No: 983   By: Helen Radcliffe (Aged 16)   From: Stoke
Climsland**

More Adults' Poems

Love is giving up watching the football to go shopping,
Love is washing up without being asked,
Love is remembering birthdays and other special days,
Love is providing a shoulder to cry on.
No: 984   By: Raymond RJ   From: London

Love is letting him watch the motor racing when you favourite soap is on,
Love is picking up his disgusting muddy socks,
Love is remembering to buy his football magazine,
Love is giving him a hug when he comes home soaking.
No: 985   By: Christina   From: London

Will you be my Valentine?
No, well never mind.
I'll by myself some flowers and a box of chocolates,
Indulge myself instead.
No: 986   By: Christina   From: London

Forget the hearts and roses instead give me an intelligent man anytime,
One who will smile at my lame jokes,
One who will invest his time in me, and not just the contents of his
wallet.
No: 987   By: Christina   From: London

Did I realize just how important you were to me my friend?
Your loyalty and your honesty,
You would never let me be less than my best,
Which surely is true love?
No: 988   By: Jean   From: Bath

A baby,
Looking surprised,
Just arrived,
God's gift of love to humankind.
No: 989   By: Felicity W.   From: Taunton

What can you say?
Nothing,
Except thank you,
For the child you know you will always love.
No: 990   By: Felicity W.   From: Taunton

I'm so proud to be your wife.
 You were,
 And always will be,
'The Love of my Life'
No: 991   By: Elizabeth   From: Tavistock

A hug is all you need
To show someone you care.
Loving thoughts and tenderness,
Is what we love to share.
No: 992   By: Barry   From: Tavistock

Nuzzling nose,
Padded toes,
Love my dog,
-Puppy love.
No: 993   By: Pip   From: Tavistock

I love cows,
With their soulful, doleful eyes,
Steamy breath,
And a heavy gentleness.
No: 994   By: Lily   From: Salisbury

I know I made you happy,
I know I made you glad,
You were such a happy chappy,
And now you're gone, I'm sad.
No: 995   By: E.C.   From: Tavistock

Bees, butterflies and birds,
Happy chirping sounds,
These make me happy,
As well as loving words.
No: 996   By: Katherine   From: Tavistock

Love me tenderly,
Love me true,
Love me always,
As I love you.
No: 997   By: Elizabeth   From: Tavistock

Red, yellow, green and blue, these are primary colours,
Mix them on a palette; paint them on the sky,
Wait for the rain and then the sun,
To have a lovely, lovely rainbow.
No: 998   By: Harry W   From: Tavistock

Rich red, good to eat,
Seeds for salad days,
The tomato,
The 'Love apple'
No: 999   By: PW   From: Tavistock

Love gives us hope,
It inspires us to do great things,
It comforts us when our lives seem unliveable,
Love is our greatest God given gift.
No: 1000   By: Anon   From: Tavistock

Little Angel, you came to my life,
You were here, and then, you were gone,
We were never destined to meet,
But, I know that we are still bonded by love.
No: 1001   By: Mum   From: Tavistock

I know that you still love me,
For I see it in your eyes,
And although now sometimes your mind wanders,
You were once so very wise.
No: 1002   By: EC   From: Tavistock

Where's the little boy gone
Whose hand I used to hold,
you were such a troubled soul,
But love has helped you to unfold.
No: 1003   By: Elle C.   From: Tavistock

A cotton wool cloud,
A gentle breeze,
Carry my love across the seas of life,
To shores unseen.
No: 1004   By: FF   From: Tavistock

More Poems from Tavistock College

(In the end) Love is pointless, a waste of time,
You get so far just to fall on your face,
Love is a game that no one can win
and in the end your heart is in pieces.
No: 1005   By: Alex Meyer   (Aged 14, 10B)

Putting on someone else's face so you will notice me,
Pretending to be someone I'm not to impress you
This infatuation is blinding me because I can't see
That making you love me is making me hate myself.
No: 1006   By: Rose Packer   (Aged 14, 10B)

I like food. I love eating.
Doughnuts are nice things, buns with icing,
Cars made from cakes freshly baked,
Burger Kings good, bacon double cheese mmm.
No: 1007   By: O. Walters Meyer   (Year 9)

She's there when I sleep, She's there when I wake,
She's there when I weep, I hope we never break,
She's there when I smile, she's there when I hate.
Will I love again or is she may fate.
No: 1008   By: Ben O'Neill   (Year 10)

Up on a tor on the moor, feet on the floor,
Through the fresh air, I stare,
Not an imperfection in sight, not a cloud in the night,
As I stand on a tor in the middle of the moor.
No: 1009   By: Dave Richards   (Year 10)

(Into the Dawn) Nature surrounds us, grasping and entangling,
The power of life in its purest form,
Amidst the dark night and into the dawn,
Follow the light, Embrace the Love.
No: 1010   By: Mark Henderson   (Year 10D)

I love Jesus,
He is the shinning one,
He shows me light where there is dark,
I am no longer sacred.
No: 1011   By: John Harley   (Year 10DA)

(Suicidal Marmite) What is the purpose
of an empty jar of Marmite?
Does it bring back memories
of that once full, once loved jar of Marmite?
No: 1012   By: Louis Wilson   (Year 10G)

Can't you see, it's not the way
Why we all fall down, it will be too late
Why is there no reason, we can't change
Why we all fall down, who will take the blame?
No: 1013   By: Ryan Bragg   (Year 9T)

Those fields near by have words written in stone,
"My love will not die please let it be known,"
This place is dead, it echoes through the town,
But I'll still have you so I will say aloud "RIP".
No: 1014   By: Callum Coley   (Aged 14)

(The Game) The rush I feel when I play the game
is the way we play as a team
the enjoyment of the game is ours to play
This is they way life is played
No: 1015   By: Alex Lecerf   (Aged 14)

Life without love is like a bap without bacon,
I once thought I felt it but I was mistaken.
But then I decided that I would go veggie
So I would describe myself as a potato wedgie
No: 1016   By: Poppy Clark & Richard Coker   (Aged 14)

I love Silence, total Silence
no gossip, no headaches, no words.
I shut my brain down into silence.
Listening to no-one, no-one to listen.
No: 1017   By: Jess Batten   (Aged 13)

Ribena, Ribena, I love Ribena,
Wendy and I love Ribena,
Katrina is our best friend,
She loves Ribena too.
No: 1018   By: Stephen Price   (Year 9)

Love is an aspiration for many,
And many more a waste of time,
I'll stick with you to the end of the world,
In hope you will be mine.
No: 1019   By: Jade Collins   (Aged 13)

An uncontrollable emotion,
Which fills our very hearts,
It's even in the air that surrounds us,
Love is everything.
No: 1020   By: Jessica Quinn   (Aged 13)

Love is a feeling an emotion we have,
Jesus showed it when he died, to save us,
You give love today, you give love tomorrow,
Sometimes you give love without even knowing.
No: 1021   By: Katherine Melville   (Aged 13)

Love can make you feel good and crazy
Love is an uncontrollable emotion that no one can live without
When you feel all warm inside, you know it's true
Just go for it, don't let it pass you.
No: 1022   By: Sophie Trudgill   (Aged 13)

Every corner I turn I hope he'll be there,
My heart loves him so much I can't fight it,
No one could tell me they love someone more,
All I want is him, in my heart, with me.
No: 1023   By: Claire Fraser   (Aged 12)

Love is an amazing emotion,
Filled with beauty and power,
Felt in many ways,
which grows by the hour.
No: 1024   By: Beth Kingman   (Aged 13)

Music can lead and I can follow
Music can change lives and it can make them,
Music has led and followed me,
Music has been there when no one else was.
No: 1025   By: James Brean   (Aged 12)

Love is a strong feeling
It can be big or small
It is up to you
Just let your imagination run wild
No: 1026   By: Lauren Evans   (Aged 12)

(Promises, Answers) It's where it starts here, outside waiting in the cold
Kiss me once in the Snow, feelings never grow old.
I promised you, I would make it warmer next year,
But can you promise me you'll still be here.
No: 1027   By: J. Woodhouse   (Aged 15)

(Colour) It lives in the sky, the petals and leaves,
It's everything we see,
A splash of colour in that shy smile,
What else could make a feeling so real?
No: 1028   By: Rachael Williams   (Aged 15)

When I'm sad, I see you strong,
What registers inside?
Why can't you hear me scream? Watch my tears,
A loveless look to life, an empty melody.
No: 1029   By: Kirsty Woodward   (Aged 15)

I loved you when I was young, you were always there,
We played, and laughed, I made you smile.
Now I try so hard to make you proud,
Why can't you see, who I'm trying to be?
No: 1030   By: Clara Wood   (Aged 14)

(My love) When you're in the open gliding, riding across water,
She reaches, grabs you lifts you up, up, 2ft, 5ft,
10ft, until it falls back, back into the wave,
She repeats it until the wind dies down, and you leave
No: 1031   By: Sam Sills   (Aged 14)

Love is like a Continuous wave, ever ongoing,
from the ocean Depths it begins,
The ups and downs of a swirling Eddy,
only to Crash against the beaten shore.
No: 1032   By: F. Edgley   (Aged 15)

My love doesn't fall into words
No: 1033   By: Leah Roberts   (Aged 15)

Love is when you feel special
It is when you have a passion
for an object, a sport or a person
This feeling can only be explained as love
No: 1034   By: Ryan Smith   (Aged 14)

Can't you see love is all around,
It's a bleeding pain which pierces your heart,
It's running around in circles for you
to help you find your perfect match soon
No: 1035   By: Kerry Horwood   (9FA)

We never have it much in the west,
But when it does the fun begins.
The ground is covered in a great white blanket
The sun can't be seen – the blanket is frightening.
No: 1036   By: Jack Litherland   (Aged 14)

Sleeping is my passion, I love it more than fashion,
through the day or night, whether it's dark or light,
Cuddled up with my furry pink teddy,
did you know his name is Fredy!
No: 1037   By: Ione Georgakis   (Aged 14)

(Kids) Cheery, knocking and party popping, always going,
never stopping, running, shouting, jumping, screaming,
never doing always dreaming, pushing, fighting, punch and slap,
but being a kid ain't all about that.
No: 1038   By: Ione Georgakis   (Aged 14)

Let's make a meal,
with a healthy feel ,
Let's make a snack,
With chef Bradley Crack.
No: 1039   By: Lesi (Aged 13) and Bradley   (Aged 14)

Comforting and creamy – Yum, Yum, Yummy
can mend a broken heart
all your worries melt away with the taste
it's a shame my love melted away so quickly.
No: 1040   By: Chloë Boka & Katy Bennett   (Aged 13)

There are many different types of love
between a girl and a boy
but if they stick together throughout all the pain
then it will bring joy
No: 1041   By: Jasmine Warne   (Aged 12)

Follow your dreams follow your heart,
Find the path that makes you smart,
Find your meaning find your Love,
Because that is what makes us, us.
No: 1042   By: Lauren Pike   (Aged 12)

Love is a glorious feeling
it strikes you when you least expect
it crawls up into your body
so you can feel the effect
No: 1043   By: Conor Hall   (Aged 13)

His ocean blue eyes looking back at me,
His rough fingers entwined with mine,
His soft brown hair brushed my cheek,
Just three simple words I can say, I love him.
No: 1044   By: Fiona McCall   (Aged 12)

Love is an important thing in everybodys life
People can find it easily
Others rather hard
Some people take advantage, others are quite nice.
No: 1045   By: Chris Wilkie   (Aged 13)

Love changes everything
Love is in the air
Love changes every one
Love is always there
No: 1046   By: David Watkins   (Aged 13)

Love is something special,
Love is everywhere,
Love is something special,
It's floating in the air.
No: 1047   By: Hannah Cole   (Aged 13)

Love is all around you know when it's there.
You get butterflies in your belly.
And Love hearts coming out of your hair
But only the right person knows when it's there.
No: 1048   By: Bethany Jade Dower   (Aged 13)

Love comes in all sorts of forms,
whether it's big or small,
you should love people for who they are
not what they look like.
No: 1049   By: Kelly Walker   (Aged 12)

Everyone loves their pets,
Dogs, cats, mammals or reptiles,
Pets love you,
Just as much as you love them.
No: 1050   By: Mark Harris   (Aged 13)

Love is not a game,
The people that play end up losing,
Others who are blameless get hurt,
And their hearts are slowly breaking.
No: 1051   By: Daniella Thyer   (Aged 13)

More Adults' Poems

If God is Love then equally, Love is God
Where two or three in God's name meet,
Their faith cannot a mountain move
But can create someone who can
No: 1052   By: John Tunnicliffe   From: Tavistock

I loved you once I love you now,
God knows I should forget
Where are you now, you haunt me still,
I'm ever glad we met.
No: 1053   By: John Tunnicliffe   From: Tavistock

Walk across the square and through the Church South Porch.
Stop and sense tranquility, which oozes from the walls
looked after all those countless years to be a place where
we may come and hear the teaching words of LOVE.
No: 1054   By: S.E.N   From: Tavistock

(V1) When I see your lovely face again,
Your smile your touch I won't refrain.
Remember the day on the digger and fishing,
But for now IL hold, wait keep wishing.
No: 1055   By: S. Rogers   From: Tavistock

(V2) I love you son you're funny and clever,
Remember IL love you forever and ever,
We will dig and fish again one day,
And in my heart you'll always stay. I LOVE YOU.
No: 1056   By: S. Rogers   From: Tavistock

(Pew Prayer 1) Thinking of others so far and so near.
Singing with neighbours; just sitting here.
Praying for resolution whether sadness, war, strife.
Being; most important, for this next week of life.
No: 1057   By: Ellie Madden-Crooby   From: Bridport

(Pew Prayer 2) How many people have sat on this place?
(Smooth wooden seat and familiar polish smells.)
What were their lives?
I try to get something of them through my coat.
No: 1058   By: Ellie Madden-Crooby   From: Bridport

(Pew Prayer 3) Quiet dark sanctuary with often spoke words.
Serene stone, polish infused wood. Home of quietude.
Sweet shop coloured light falls into bright flowers
And singing in frequent celebrations bursts out of here.
No: 1059   By: Ellie Madden-Crooby   From: Bridport

You know I love you
I'll stay true to you
Until such a day
When my heart gets snapped away
No: 1060   By: Astrid Fisher   From: Plymouth

If this love is to survive
Then keep the dream alive
The dream in which the two of us are friends
Within a romance that never ends
No: 1061   By: Astrid Fisher   From: Plymouth

Of all the blessings that God has showered upon us,
Love is the most precious,
Often invisible,
It is the small still voice that binds all human-kind.
No: 1062   By: MIF   From: Tavistock

Let not your lonely heart dispel the joyful moments past
Or mists of time cloud tender memories meant to last
Vanities slowly fade while gentle feelings linger on
Everlasting treasured thoughts, remembering one who's gone.
No: 1063   By: Ian Jenkins   From: Tavistock